Blueprint i... presen-
tation of th... he bib-
lical doctri... ...., and redemption. Kent
DelHousaye does an excellent job of weaving important themes
together into an integrated narrative that is easy to read without
being simplistic. In a day when more and more Christians are
not thinking through the implications of central biblical doc-
trines, *Blueprint in Bedlam* provides a refreshing anecdote.

JP MORELAND, DISTINGUISHED PROFESSOR OF PHILOSOPHY
TALBOT SCHOOL OF THEOLOGY, BIOLA UNIVERSITY

A clear, concise, and well written treatment of 'old truths' that
have been neglected or forgotten at great cost to today's Christians. Kent writes with a fresh insight and contemporary application that caused me to do more than a few double takes on
these familiar passages in Genesis. Rarely do I find such solid
scholarship with practical application. I highly recommend Kent
and his book to you.

CHIP INGRAM, TEACHING PASTOR OF LIVING
ON THE EDGE MINISTRIES; BESTSELLING AUTHOR OF
TRUE SPIRITUALITY: BECOMING A ROMANS 12 CHRISTIAN

Blueprint in Bedlam clearly and concisely speaks to one of the
biggest questions our culture is asking today: what does it mean
to be human? The doctrine of creation is foundational for Chris-
tian-worldview thinking, and Kent DelHousaye has done the
body of Christ a great service by explaining the everyday implications of being made in God's image.

JONATHAN MORROW, AUTHOR OF THINK CHRISTIANLY
FOUNDER OF WWW.THINKCHRISTIANLY.ORG

Kent DelHousaye's book, *Blueprint in Bedlam*, is filled with perceptive insights into the human heart and frequent wise applications of the Bible to everyday life. This is an enjoyable, interesting, insightful treatment of many of the 'big questions' that everybody needs to answer about God and the meaning of human life.

WAYNE GRUDEM, RESEARCH PROFESSOR OF THEOLOGY
AND BIBLICAL STUDIES, PHOENIX SEMINARY, AZ

Who are we? and *What is the meaning of life?* are the age-old questions that for centuries plagued people's minds, but the answers to them always satisfy the soul. Through a combination of strong scholarship, compelling illustrations, relevant applications, and clear explanations, Kent DelHousaye draws the reader back to theological foundations grounded in Scripture to uncover the answers. *Blueprint in Bedlam* is an easy-to-read book for the everyday person that's needed for a time such as ours. As a pastor and artist in Los Angeles, this book strengthened my development.

BRIAN S. CHAN, PASTOR, WRITER, AND ARTIST IN HOLLYWOOD
PROFESSOR AT BIOLA UNIVERSITY; AUTHOR OF *THE PURPLE CURTAIN*

BLUEPRINT
IN
BEDLAM

BLUEPRINT
IN
BEDLAM

GOD'S
PLAN
AMID THE
CHAOS

KENT MICHAEL DELHOUSAYE

BLUEPRINT IN BEDLAM
© 2014 by Kent DelHousaye

All rights reserved. No part of this book may be reproduced or transmitted in any form or by any means, electronic or mechanical, including photocopying and recording, or by any information storage and retrieval system, without permission in writing from the publisher.

Scripture quotations are from The Holy Bible, English Standard Version, copyright © 2001 by Crossway Bibles, a division of Good News Publishers. Used by permission. All rights reserved.

Deep River Books
Sisters, Oregon
www.deepriverbooks.com

ISBN – 13: 9781940269115
ISBN – 10: 1940269113

Library of Congress: 2014930278

Printed in the USA

Cover design by Jason Enterline

To my beloved bride, Stephanie,
and
children Ethan, Christian, and Claire

&

CONTENTS

INTRODUCTION

George Gaylord Simpson, who was perhaps the most influential evolutionary paleontologist of the twentieth century, once callously and bluntly stated that "Man is the result of a purposeless and natural process that did not have him in mind."[1] It was his belief that there is nothing especially unique about human beings. They are simply one of the many accidental developments of history, and blind chance is the only reason people even exist in the world today.

Given the prevalence of this belief in our day, is it any wonder that people seem to be more lost and miserable than ever? Despite living at the apex of human progress and achievement, our sense of purpose appears to be at an all-time low. Depression, anxiety, and anger are rampant in our culture today, and people are increasingly turning to substances, violence, and suicide to cope with their hopelessness. The reality is that we are struggling more than ever with significance and meaning in this life, and I would suggest that the cold evolutionary science we are force-fed today is much to blame for it.

Evolutionary science tells us that people don't matter, and the reason we don't matter is that we were not made with intent by a loving Creator. Rather, we are simply the most advanced animal species to evolve in a long chain of accidental events. We are told that we have no inherent value and no inalienable purpose. And the inevitable result is a planet full of people who have no idea where they come from, why they are here, or where they are going. And people who don't know who they are become desperate and perhaps even dangerous people.

From a young age, we are taught that human beings are really nothing more than a "chance configuration of atoms in the slip stream of meaningless chance history."[2] When we start to believe this, then we lose our sense of direction, purpose, and dignity. And when we lose these things, we lose ourselves. We lose our identity as unique and valuable beings who have been carefully and purposefully made in the image of the Creator.

The first three chapters of Genesis are perhaps the most important three chapters in the Bible for the simple reason that they tell us who we are. They answer the most fundamental questions about life and tell us not just that God created us but how and why he did it. They introduce God's intentions for humanity, explain what happened when we sinned against him, and reveal God's plans to heal and restore us. They are the blueprint that explains life as we see it unfolding around us.

The story of creation is, therefore, the foundational story for us, and it starts with the fact that God made us all. Understanding the fundamental difference between Creator and creation is the starting point for appreciating God's purposes for the human race—and for each one of us individually. Once we really get the idea that the God of the universe created us and that we are not the inevitable result of blind chance, then we can actually start to grasp his purposes for this world and our lives.

Knowing that we are not accidental but intentional is the key to accessing meaning, significance, and identity. For this reason, we must regain what has largely been lost in the last century. That is, we have to reclaim the simple truth that has been widely discarded about people—that we are made in the image of God, we have great value, and we exist for a divinely appointed purpose.

This book is about finding real meaning and significance in

the story of creation. We live in an age that tells us there is no intention or design for the world and that nothing really matters or lasts in the grand scheme of things. But that just isn't true. Everybody and everything matters because nobody and nothing is an accident. God made it all, and he made it for a purpose. Consider this an invitation to read on and find out just what that purpose is.

CHAPTER 1

GOD'S BLUEPRINT FOR OUR WORLD

The famed English journalist G.K. Chesterton once wrote, "It is absurd for the evolutionist to complain that it is unthinkable for an admittedly unthinkable God to make everything out of nothing, and then pretend that it is *more* thinkable that nothing should turn itself into everything."[3] Chesterton was right. It is absurd to think that everything that is in existence has developed by random chance rather than by purposeful design. The truth is that there is so much order, complexity, symmetry, and proportion in the universe that it, in reality, takes greater faith to believe that the world is an accident than to believe that there is a Creator behind it.

Consider, for example, Charles Darwin's take on the origin and meaning of crying. The father of modern evolutionary theory described the act as simply being "an incidental result, as purposeless as the secretion of tears from a blow outside the eye."[4] Now, even nonsentimentalists would agree that weeping is much more than just purposeless eye secretions. No, crying has meaning. It reveals a host of emotions that we are capable of expressing, and it would be callous and simplistic to deny that. This is apparent to most of us; and yet, for some reason it's absurdly evasive for evolutionists. What seems obvious to you and me is not obvious for them—that we are much more than robotic machines or advanced animals who weep only because we have water in our eyes.

Those who [...]
series of accident[...]
of a Designer are [...]
lished and unive[...]
is that a fundame[...]
ment. Evolution [...]
origins. That is, [...]
the origin of th[...]
evolutionary pr[...]
the universe act[...]

Everything [...]
all things have [...]
have a clear answer to the question of [...]
us that "in the beginning God created." There really is no confusion about the origin of all things for those of us who accept the explanation that the Bible provides. The burden of proof is upon those who don't. Their burden is to explain how everything came into being on its own without any cause or interference from some preexistent divine being. They have to find a way to come up with an answer to adequately explain how everything got its start by itself.

Keep in mind that many have tried. Most recently, Stephen Hawking published his argument for the nonnecessity of a Creator in his controversial book *The Grand Design*. His book caused quite a stir among scientists and religious leaders alike because he dared attempt to explain the origins question away by simply dismissing the need for God. He wrote that "It is not necessary to invoke God to light the blue touch paper and set the universe going."[5] Like Hawking, other evolutionists have proposed all kinds of explanations for the origin of the universe, developing and promoting theories such as the big bang, quantum mechanics, and cosmic inflation. And yet none of these theories has really answered the fundamental issue, which is that something or someone had to initiate all of these events. There had to be a First Cause.

The only really viable explanation for the origin of the universe is that there is an uncaused First Cause. This cause cannot be an immaterial thing that has no cognition, volition, or power, for inanimate things have no reason or motive to move, and they certainly have no purpose for doing so. Rather, this First Cause must be something or someone who is supernatural, free-willed, and intelligent. It must be a being who has the authority, the knowledge, and the will to act. As Chesterton said, it is simply incoherent to argue that chance and necessity by themselves can set the universe into motion, and do it by accident no less. The truth is that nothing cannot turn itself into something. No, something or somebody must bring it into being.

As Christians, we believe that this First Cause is the God of the Bible. In Genesis 1 we read that God created everything, and it says that he did it in the beginning. The Hebrew word in the first verse for created is the word *barah,* which means "to form or shape." So Genesis 1:1 says that in the beginning it was God who formed and shaped the universe. It was God who caused the chain of creation events and brought order out of cosmic chaos. This is important because the text itself tells us that up until that event, the universe was formless and shapeless. In other words, it had no form or shape until God gave it.

This is significant because many people today think that things evolved naturally through long transitional processes. They believe this and take it at face value because it is all they have ever heard. They have been repeatedly told by their teachers, their textbooks, and their experts that the development of nature and life was essentially the outcome of a series of accidents, but the Scriptures tell us it was anything but accidental.

Genesis tells us that everything was intentionally and purposefully created by a Creator. After many years, science is beginning to catch up with Scripture, as Intelligent Design is starting to take hold as not only a viable but also a compelling theory.

What is Intelligent Design? It is the theory that suggests there is overwhelming evidence of design, order, symmetry, and proportion in the universe, both at the macrocosmic and microcosmic levels. There is compelling evidence of design at work in the organization of vast constellations as well as in the organization of the simple cell. Throughout nature and in every field of study, including physics, mathematics, and astronomy, the evidence of intelligence at work is astounding. Proponents of Intelligent Design argue that this complexity clearly points us to the existence of a Designer. William Paley's famous watchmaker argument is regularly cited as an effective argument for natural theology because it demonstrates that there must be a watchmaker behind every watch. According to this argument, the existence of a watch necessitates the prior existence of an intelligent maker. After all, watches do not and cannot make themselves.

Some have likened the study of natural theology to finding a grand piano being washed up on a sea shore. No one who found such a thing would presume that it had somehow incidentally formed in the ocean over time. That would be absurd. Instead, they would conclude that it had fallen off a boat or been dumped there intact because pianos don't make themselves. No matter how much time passes, a grand piano cannot come together by accident. The keys don't carve themselves, the pedals don't insert themselves, and the strings don't stretch themselves. There is far too much evidence of order, design, and purpose in a piano to just ignore it. Surely, there must have been an intelligent and skilled piano maker.

Genesis says that God is the First Cause who caused and created everything. How did he do it? He spoke. We read that "God said...let there be." So God spoke or breathed things into existence. Now, when Genesis says that God spoke, it doesn't mean that he speaks just like we do. No, this is what is called an anthropomorphism, which is assigning a human quality to God for our own understanding. When God speaks, he doesn't issue words as we do, unless he uses the voice of an angel or some other being to do so. Rather, God speaks by breathing his will into existence.

In this case, God "spoke" things into existence in an instant over the course of six creation days. What we see in the account is that things appeared instantly at his command. They did not appear progressively or over the course of time. Rather, things came into being at the moment he spoke them into existence. Is there any evidence for cosmically instantaneous events like these? Recently, I came across a newspaper article that featured the work of Dr. Charles Bennett, a respected physicist who presented research at Princeton University that proves the universe grew to astounding proportions in less than the blink of an eye. By measuring the faint cosmic glow of the oldest known light in the universe, he and his fellow physicists have found what they call "smoking gun" evidence that the universe expanded from the size of a marble in less than a trillionth of a second.[6]

Dr. Bennett's research actually aligns with and confirms what the Bible teaches us, that the universe came into being in an instantaneous event. The question is what or who caused that event? Simply put, God did. What scientists call the big bang, we call the creation event. The universe came into being at once, and only God could have pulled it off. Hebrews 11:3 says, "By faith we understand that the universe was created by the word of God, so that what is seen was not made out of things that are visible." The theological term *ex nihilo* means "out from nothing," and it describes how everything actually came from nothing. The problem is that nothing cannot create something. That is logically impossible. Only someone intelligent, powerful, and creative can make something out of nothing. The author of Hebrews tells us that God is the one who made all things, for only he has the creative capacity to turn nothing into everything.

The Bible tells us that God created everything, and it also tells us how and why he did it. The author of Genesis says that God "made" everything. The Hebrew word for made is *asah*, which literally means "carefully fashioned." It is possible that one can create something and do it in a careless and thoughtless way, but the language suggests that God did nothing of the sort. Rather, God put a lot of thought and creative energy into everything he created. God created everything with thoughtful care. Because God did this, everything he made is valuable and purposeful.

Take our tears, for example. God considered putting tear ducts into our eyes not just for physical purposes but for emotional ones too. Tears, of course, do serve the rudimentary purpose of cleaning our eyes, but they also serve a much more sophisticated purpose, which is to express our emotions. God put such thought into us as to give us the means to express how we feel both in joy and in grief. We cry when we're happy, and we cry when we're sad. Sometimes we cry when we're neither happy nor sad. This ability is evidence of God's consideration of us. God created you and me with thoughtful care, and he has shown us his care in the way that he has carefully fashioned and equipped us as human beings.

Scientists have rightly noted the difference between humans and most animals, which lack the ability to cry. Though there are some noted exceptions (such as elephants and chimpanzees), their weeping is far less complicated than ours and usually only happens when a member of the herd or the family dies. Our ability to express a range of emotions through tears is not found in the animal kingdom because it is something uniquely endowed in us. You and I have been given a capacity by God that clearly and powerfully exhibits just how much thought and care God put into making us.

In 1 Timothy 4:4 Paul wrote that "Everything created by God is good," and in Ephesians 2:10 that "We are his workmanship, created in Christ Jesus for good works." The word "good" is often equated with God's creation, and this is not just a statement about value but also about purpose. When God called everything "good," he was declaring that everything he had made was purposeful and intentional. That is, every single thing that God makes is, by design, divinely and carefully superintended. There is nothing in God's creation that is too small or too insignificant to be part of his plan. No, every single thing that God has made is important and meaningful.

The author of Genesis tells us that God thoughtfully and carefully fashioned all things. He made the light, the darkness, the water, the land, the plants, the sun, the moon, the stars, the animals, and of course, the human beings. He made them all, and he made them glorious. The poet Elizabeth Barrett Browning echoed this truth so eloquently when she wrote "Earth's crammed with heaven, and every common bush aflame with God."[7] And the poet W.H. Auden voiced the same when he wrote that, "Even the most commonplace things are tinged with glory."[8] Even into the most simple things, God put much thought and care, and as such they bear his glory, even if just a tinge.

So why did God do it? Why did he invest so much care and thought into his creation? The answer is that God poured himself into his creation because it made him happy. God made everything for his own pleasure. Just as it says in Genesis that God made everything, it also says that he "saw" everything. As soon as God made the things he created, we read that he surveyed them. The Hebrew word for "saw" is *raah,* and it means "to gaze or look upon." It does not suggest casting a simple glance or taking a quick look. Rather, it suggests taking something in and drinking deeply from it. When it says that God saw all that he created, it means that he took great pleasure in the glory of the things he carefully and purposefully fashioned.

This is a lot like building something and then stopping once in a while to take in what you've accomplished. I recently built a play set in my backyard for my children. It was a big project that took me a few days and required a lot of sweat, but I took regular breaks from my work each day and gave myself time to "see" what I had accomplished. As the set began to take shape, I swelled with pleasure as I pictured the faces of my kids when they would see it and the fun they would have when they played on it. My excitement increased with each step, and my anticipation grew as the project neared completion. When it was finished, I actually spent several minutes just taking it all in and admiring the fruit of my own labor. In other words, I was pleased and satisfied with my work.

When God stopped each day to see what he had created, he took the same kind of pleasure from and satisfaction in his work. Genesis says that God looked and saw "that it was good." The Hebrew word for good is *tov,* which means "pleasing or beautiful." The word used here to describe God's impression of the things he created suggests that there is something inherently pleasing and beautiful about each created thing. God clearly admired his handiwork because each thing that he made, be it the stars, the ocean, or the people he created, was good. And good does not mean simply that God liked them. It means that God recognized the inherent goodness and beauty of all the things he had carefully and purposefully made.

There is a fascinating debate occurring today about the nature of what is good and beautiful. Beauty, for example, is often defined as "in the eye of the beholder," and we are largely influenced by our culture to presume that beauty is a completely subjective standard. In fact, we are almost offended at the concept that anything could be considered objectively beautiful. And yet we see in the creation story that there is such a thing as objective beauty. When Genesis says that God made everything good, it implies that whatever God made is inherently beautiful. One would be hard-pressed to make the case that there is nothing that is truly objectively beautiful, at least in its initial created form.

It is true that sin has corrupted that beauty, however. When Adam and Eve sinned at the fall, they brought ruin and corruption not only upon themselves but also upon all of creation. And yet no one knows just how tainted and corrupted everything became. Most Bible scholars agree that sin corrupted the earth, but they disagree on just how much. Many think that original sin seared much of what is beautiful in creation and some think it merely singed it, but few of them seem to think that sin has completely destroyed it. No, sin has not changed the intrinsic goodness of the world that God has created. Though sin may damage the beauty of goodness, it does not snuff it out. There is simply too much evidence in the world and in Scripture to deny that there is still much that is good and beautiful about God's creation. One only has to gaze at a desert sunset, a crystal blue lake, or a majestic mountaintop to recognize that there is still goodness and beauty in our world. We only need to smell the fragrance of a spring flower, hear the music of birds chirping in the morning, or listen to the waves crashing on the sea to realize that there is beauty in God's creation still. And here's the thing. We can all agree on this, even if we do not share the same background, experience, or belief. Even if we share almost nothing else in common, we can share a common appreciation for that which is beautiful. People from all walks and times can actually agree on what is beautiful, and very few, if any at all, would make the case that roses stink or that sunrises are ugly. I also don't know anyone who would argue that Bach and Mozart made terrible music or that newborn babies aren't cute and sweet.

In a survey I conducted with my church, I asked my congregation if they believed in objective beauty, and I found that only 70 percent of the adults and just 35 percent of the teens did. I pastor a well-respected and established Bible church. My congregation is theologically conservative and biblically literate, and yet many of them don't believe or just don't understand the nature of objective beauty. Nor do they appreciate the importance of it. I suspect it is not much different in other churches. *The fact that God made and declared everything beautiful is significant because it provides the foundation for dignity and worth not only for people but for the world in which we live.* If we fail to respect the intrinsic beauty of the people, the things, and the world that God has created, then we will lose our hold on even more important virtues like goodness and truth.

I recently listened to an amazing lecture by Dr. John Mark Reynolds, the founder and director of the Torrey Honors Institute at Biola University and professor of philosophy, who spoke about the immense import of knowing and defending objective beauty.[9] In his lecture he made the case that a civilization starts to decline once it loses its sense of objective beauty. He argued that if we lose hold of our sense of objective beauty, then what necessarily follows is a loss of goodness and then truth. In other words, our consensus about what is objectively or inherently beautiful provides the foundation for agreement on what is good and true. If we stop agreeing on what is truly beautiful, then we have no reason not to disagree about what is good and true. The end result is a world in which there is no fundamental sense of any overarching truth or reality.

You can probably imagine how this not only feeds but satisfies the postmodernism of our time. At the heart of postmodern thought is the belief that there is no metanarrative or grand story for all people. All we really have are our own cultural stories and our own personal, subjective truths that we ought not impose on others. We live in a world in which everyone's competing claims on goodness and truth are equally respected. This pluralistic kind of thinking has its origination in the slowly dissolving sense of objective beauty. If we stop to think about it, the unraveling agreement on what is fundamentally beautiful does indeed lead to the dismantling of fundamental goodness and truth.

Solomon wrote in Ecclesiastes 3:11, "[God] has made everything beautiful in its time." We often focus in on the "in its time" part of this verse as it relates to God's timing in life, but the more important portion of the verse is what precedes it. The Scripture says that God has made everything beautiful! The implication is that God does not make anything ugly. Everything that God has made is beautiful and pleasing to him, even though it is marred by sin. God has instilled beauty and goodness into everything that he has made and finds pleasure in all these things. And if creation is beautiful and pleasing to God, then creation should also be beautiful and pleasing to us. This means we ought to recognize the fundamental, intrinsic beauty of all God's creation.

The English journalist Malcolm Muggeridge once wrote, "Every happening, great and small, is a parable whereby God speaks to us, and the art of life is to get the message."[10] His point is that God has communicated an important message to humanity, a message about God's pleasure in and purposes for creation. Even though our culture tells us that everything and everyone is just a cosmic accident, the truth is that there is a loving Creator behind it all who infused both pleasure and purpose into every thing and every creature he made. There is a God who lovingly fashioned everything for a grand purpose and who is writing an overarching story in the world that he created. You and I are in this story, and that means we are part of God's master plan and ultimate purpose for the world we live in. We each have a role to play and a purpose to fulfill in the metanarrative of life. Therefore, it's critical that we all understand our place in God's story.

Just a short time ago I was sitting in a meeting of the Evangelical Philosophical Society listening to the late Dr. Dallas Willard give a lecture about how people are losing their bearings on what is true and good. He lamented the fact that people have forgotten their story. They've forgotten where they've come from, why they are here, and where they are going. They have no sense of their place in the story of history and are completely oblivious to God's intentions for them. People are losing their identity because they've forgotten the great story of creation. They have forgotten that they were carefully fashioned by a Creator who thinks they are beautiful and delights in them. This is why it is so important to tell and retell this story, to remind the world there really is a God, a God who created and loves and has plans for all things.

DISCUSSION QUESTIONS

1. What is the Achilles' heel of evolutionary theory? Why?

2. What is Intelligent Design? Why is it a viable explanation for the universe?

3. What means did God use to create the world? Was it an event or a process?

4. How did God create everything? What does that say about value and purpose?

5. Why did God create everything? What does that say about beauty and goodness?

CHAPTER 2
GOD'S BLUEPRINT FOR OUR LIVES

Near the end of his life, the famous atheist Jean-Paul Sartre apparently had a change of heart and confessed to his friend Pierre Victor (aka Benny Levy): "I do not feel that I am the product of chance, a speck of dust in the universe, but someone who was expected, prepared, pre-figured. In short, a being whom only a Creator could put here; and this idea of a creating hand refers to God."[11] Sartre's deathbed confession was a stark change for a man who was one of the world's most outspoken atheists during his time. Sartre was an unapologetic naturalist who for most of his life believed that there was no Creator and that everything came to be by deterministic chance. And yet his senses apparently came to him at the end of his life as he embraced the idea that there was indeed an Intelligent Creator who carefully and thoughtfully made him.

The best-selling author Nevada Barr wrote about her own awakening to this critical truth in her book *Seeking Enlightenment Hat by Hat: A Skeptic's Path to Religion*. She wrote, "It was a number of years of crashing and burning in the personal arena before I made the discovery that I was not God. Finally I realized that though I was not God, I was *of* God."[12] It took her many years to figure out that God had intentional and purposeful plans for her life. Yet, when she did, it was monumental for her own sense of meaning and identity.

The Bible tells us that God did make all of us and that he

did it for a purpose. In the first chapter of Genesis we read that God made everything. In the first five days, he made the sun, moon, and stars, and he made the land, plants, and animals. On the sixth day of creation he made people. God saved the last day of creation for his best creation. When God made people, he made them different from everything else. He made man and woman uniquely endowed with special gifts and qualities. Mankind was the pinnacle of God's creation and his greatest triumph, and he proved it in the way that he blessed them. So, what did God do for human beings that set them apart?

First, God empowered people, and he did it in two ways. God gave man two gifts that he didn't give to any other creature. The most important of these gifts is his image. In Genesis 1:26 we read, "Then God said, 'Let us make man in our image, after our likeness.'" What does that mean? It seems odd that God would say "us" and "our," doesn't it? That is, unless we understand that God exists as a triune God, which means that he is three persons in one, consisting of God the Father, God the Son, and God the Holy Spirit. When we get the tri-unity of God and the fact that all three members of the Trinity were involved in creation, then the language doesn't seem so odd. In fact, it makes perfect sense.

I was driving down the road recently and saw a bumper sticker on a car in front of me. It read "People plan, God laugh." Now, I was a journalism major back in college, so I can be bit of a grammar Nazi. Poor grammar really bugs me. So when I initially read the sticker, I was thought it was incorrect. After all, shouldn't it read "God laughs"? But then I stopped and thought about it. If God is indeed triune, then wouldn't it actually be more correct to reflect that in our grammar? Yes, of course it would! When we think about God in terms of three persons in one, then it makes sense to render that in our language.

And so it is in the Hebrew text. It makes perfect sense that God would refer to himself in the plural since he exists as three. The triune God declares in Genesis 1:26, "Let us make man in our image, after our likeness." We read that the collective Godhead agree to share their collective image with mankind, which is something quite special. The Hebrew word for "image" is *tselem*, and it means "shape, resemblance, or shadow." God actually shared his collective shape or shadow with human beings. What is most interesting is that God does not use this word to refer to any other creatures. In other words, God did not choose to share his image with any other thing. Humans are the only creatures in all creation who bear the image of God.

The simple truth that human beings are distinctly different from other creatures because they bear the image of God has enormous implications upon how we view ourselves and other people. The fact that humans, and humans only, have the image of God ought to impact how we view our own uniqueness in the created order. Whereas plants and animals have value and were created with thoughtful care and for God's pleasure just like people, they do not share the image of God like we do. This creates a significant line of separation between humans and the plant and animal species on earth. Because human beings were created in the image of God, they are not just another kind of animal. They are completely distinct if for no other reason than the fact that they have the Imago Dei.

Because you and I bear the image of God, we are unique and special in a way that no other creatures are. Though we are told often that there is nothing especially notable about us, that we are simply advanced animals who happen to walk upright, the reality is that we are much more than that. There is something divine in each one of us, an image that is a gift from our Creator to us. This image sets us apart and makes us different.

It makes us special. The truth is that to say a human being is nothing but molecules and atoms is like saying a Shakespearean play is nothing but letters and words. Because we bear God's divine image, we are the Creator's poetry. Everything else around us is just prose.

I was sitting in a lounge chair reading at a resort one day and a man noticed that I was taking in a book on Intelligent Design. He came over and asked me about it, and we struck up a conversation. It turns out the man was a biochemist who had become a Christian after being a naturalist for most of his life. He was a staunch atheist who set out to prove theism wrong with his life's work but became convinced of the existence of God by the design and order he observed in his field of study. The more he looked into the complexity of things, the more open he became to Intelligent Design. He ended up reading several books on the subject and eventually became a Christian. He now devotes much of his work to studying and teaching Intelligent Design, and he was thrilled to see me reading about it.[13]

In our conversation, this Christian biochemist told me about a genetics project he was working on, and he described how our human genetic code is so long that were it printed on paper, it would fill up over a million pages with information that would stretch more than 208 miles long when laid out end to end! He also told me that twenty-three thousand of those pages of information (or over four miles of it) is completely different from that of chimpanzees. He emphasized that the genetic difference was significant and that much of the news made about the supposed genetic similarity between modern man and primates is greatly overstated. He said that man is actually not similar at all to primates and there's no evidence that one evolved from the other.

I did some research of my own after that conversation and confirmed everything he told me that day. Even though I knew in my gut already that this was true, I had never really looked into the reasons why. It's true that much is made of the seeming genetic similarity between humans and apes, but that apparent similarity doesn't really mean much. British genetics professor Steve Jones has pointed out that we share genetic similarity with all kinds of things, but that doesn't mean we share common ancestry. In his fascinating research, for example, he found that we actually have a 60 percent genetic similarity to bananas, but that doesn't mean we are half-banana. (Some of us may be half bananas, but that's a different subject!)[14]

Not only are we biologically distinct from primates, and bananas for that matter, we are ontologically different too. To be ontologically different means to be not just quantitatively different in the number of genes we have, but qualitatively different in the type of creature that we are. As human beings, what makes us truly different from all other creatures is the image of God that we inherently bear. The Imago Dei in humanity not only makes us distinct from animals, it also sets us above them. Right after God says "Let us make man in our image," in Genesis 1:26, he declares, "And let them have dominion over the fish of the sea and over the birds of the heavens and over the livestock and over all the earth and over every creeping thing that creeps on the earth." In assigning dominion to human beings, God gives people his authority. The Hebrew word for "dominion" is *radah,* and it means "to subjugate or rule." God set people over and above the rest of his creation. This is not just priority in value and significance but priority in order. God gave people the divinely sanctioned right to rule over all the other creatures he made. In so doing, God delegated legitimate authority to people to exercise sovereignty over the rest of the created order of plants, animals, and nature.

King David in Psalm 8:6–8 wrote this of God and the authority he assigned to humans: "You have given him dominion over the works of your hands; you have put all these things under his feet, all sheep and oxen, and also the beasts of the field, the birds of the heavens, and the fish of the sea, whatever passes along the paths of the seas." Without exception, all creatures and created things are placed under the authority of man.

At the same time, notice that David says God has given us dominion over the works of "his hands," not ours. This means that though God has given us authority to rule over other creatures, that authority is not absolute. Our authority is not absolute because creation is God's work and not ours. It still belongs to him and not to us. Therefore, our authority is measured by God's will for his creation and not our own. We only rule over God's creation the way that he wants us to. Therefore, this mandate is a command to steward and not abuse or exploit the earth's resources or the creatures that live on it. The mandate of dominion is really a responsibility that has been delegated to us by God to care for and serve his creation.

At the same time, the empowerment that God gave to human beings does set them apart and above other creatures. This divine empowerment given by the Creator to mankind makes us different, and it shows just how highly God thinks of us. In fact, it shows us that he thinks more highly of people than anything else that he has made. Now, this shouldn't serve to make us prideful but rather to make us grateful. In other words, it ought to encourage us by proving to us just how valuable we are to God. Because our Maker shared his image with us, we are blessed with a level of glory and dignity that no other creatures get to enjoy.

Genesis 1:27 says, "So God created man in his own image."

In so doing, God gave people a taste of his glory. It's interesting that in 1 Corinthians 11:7, the apostle Paul wrote, "A man ought not to cover his head since he is the image and glory of God." Paul emphasizes that God made us in his image, but he adds something to the idea that is significant. He tells us that man is the image *and* glory of God. He means that bearing the Imago Dei brings not just the power of being like God, but also the glory that comes with it. This glory is the "likeness" that we share with God as human beings. Don't forget that God said, "Let us make man in our image, after our likeness." The Hebrew word for "likeness" is *demuth*, which means "copy, reproduction, or facsimile."

I have a fake one million dollar bill in my desk. It actually looks real. Though it's just silly play money, you would think it was a real bill if you didn't look too closely because it has all the distinguishing characteristics of any bill. It is green, it feels just like a regular bill, and it has many of the same numbers and designs on it. The only big difference is that it has a prominently displayed statement running across it which reads, "This bill is not a representation or facsimile of any obligation." This is helpful, especially for those of us who are prone to think there is such a thing as a million dollar bill! Of course, there is no such thing. As I write this, there is a news story about a man who tried to cash one in and went to jail for it, so that serves to prove that some people are still not convinced. However, the bill I have in my desk is not a real bill; it is just a representation or facsimile of an actual note.

As image bearers, we bear the likeness of God, which means essentially that we are copies or facsimiles of God—like a fax image. This means that God retains his image in whole, but he shares it with us in part. Though God does not make us just like him, he does make us similar to him by sharing his glory with us. The Bible tells us that God shares certain attributes and qualities with people. Theologians refer to these qualities as "communicable attributes," which means that they can be shared with or "communicated to" people. Some of the qualities that God can and does share with us are aspects of his character, his intellect, and his emotions. This means that we can think, act, and feel like God. We can think like God because we can learn, reason, and gain wisdom from him. Likewise, we can act like God by having integrity, dealing justly with others, and living creatively as he does. And in the same way, we can feel like God by being compassionate, patient, and forgiving as he is. These are just some of the many things we share with the God who made us. He has communicated the capacity to enjoy all these attributes to every human being, and that is the benefit that comes from the glory he has shared with us.

At the same time, there are other qualities or attributes that God cannot and does not share with us. Theologians, in turn, call these things "incommunicable attributes." God, for example, does not share his eternality, his immensity, or his sovereignty with us. Bible scholars talk a lot about the omnis in theology. God is omni everything. He is omnipresent, which means that he is everywhere (or everywhere is in his presence). He is omniscient, which means that he knows everything. And God is omnipotent, which means that he controls everything. All of these attributes belong to God because he is infinite, but God cannot and does not share these qualities with finite beings like us.

The fact remains, though, that there is much we share in common with God. Because God made us in his image, he has shared his glory with us. Even more, he has also shared his dignity. In Genesis 1:27 we read, "So God created man in his own image, in the image of God he created him; male and female he created them." The last phrase of that verse is quite significant because it has much to say to us about dignity and respect. Because men and women both bear the image of God, this statement in the creation account has enormous implications on our view of human dignity and worth.

First, it means that men and women are inherently equal in their value. It says that God emphatically made "male and female" in his image, so we must reject gender inequality and instead affirm the dignity of women. Today this might seem like a given, but women have for much of history been largely regarded as having less dignity and worth than their male counterparts. And in some countries of the world, they are still regarded and treated this way. Misogynistic thinking like this is not only biblically inaccurate; it is downright offensive because it flies in the face of God's dignity, which has been provided to women who bear the image of God as much as men do.

Second, it means that because God created all people in his image, they all have unqualified inherent value. This means that every human being on earth has dignity and deserves sanctity. Practically, this means that we must affirm and defend the dignity and sanctity of life for every human being. It is as C.S. Lewis said, "There are no ordinary people. You have never talked to a mere mortal."[15] Because of the Imago Dei, we really must stand for the dignity of all human beings and stand up against the various assaults on human dignity in the world, such as abortion, genocide, infanticide, euthanasia, slavery, trafficking, oppression, abuse, and neglect. All of these social plagues are a direct attack on the God-given dignity of human beings, and we should be personally offended and motivated to action by them all. The simple reason we must speak up and act out against injustices like these is that they violate the image of God in people.

The movie *October Baby* tells the story of a nineteen-year-old college student named Hannah who learns that she suffers from epilepsy because she was born as the result of a failed late-term abortion. The movie is inspired by the true life story of Gianna Jessen, who travels the world telling her story to anyone who will listen. Gianna's birth mother tried to terminate her in a botched saline abortion, in which a toxic solution is injected into the womb to poison and burn the baby from the inside out. Gianna somehow survived the experience and was adopted, but she has suffered with cerebral palsy ever since. Growing up, she learned to face not only the rejection of her birth mother, who now refers to her as an embarrassment, but also the ridicule of others who have told her she is a burden to society. Her response to those who have devalued and dehumanized her throughout her life is to remind them that she is "God's girl" and that God has told her, "I am going to define you…you are not forgotten… you are loved."

Perhaps you have suffered like Gianna. You may have been abused, neglected, or rejected by others who have made you feel like you aren't worth anything. Maybe people told you that you aren't special or that you don't have anything valuable to offer the world. They are wrong about you. They are wrong about your worth and your value. Your dignity is not tied up in who the world thinks you are, in what they like about you, or in what you have to offer them. Your dignity is grounded in the fact that you are "God's girl" or "God's boy." Let God define who you are; don't let others do it. God says you are not forgotten, and you are loved. And that has nothing to do with anything other than the fact that he has made you in his image.

In Genesis 9:6 it says that, "Whoever sheds the blood of man, by man shall his blood be shed, for God made man [male and female] in his image." As it explicitly states, God will require the life of any person who takes the life of another because to do so violates the value and significance that God has placed within that person. To kill another is to attack the very image of God in people. This means that God considers murder not just an attack on that person but an indirect assault on himself. Jesus later told us that we mentally murder others when we hold anger against them in Matthew 5:22, so the image of God in people ought not only to challenge how we treat others but also how we think about them! God has provided dignity to all human beings, and he requires us to respect and protect it.

And third, the image of God in people also provides the foundation for a healthy self-image. Self-esteem is all the rage today, but the Bible says nothing positive about esteeming one's self. The Bible calls that pride. However, the Bible does have much to say about the concept of the self-image. The most important is what it says right here in Genesis about bearing the image of God. When we recognize our own worth as image bearers, then we can start to truly appreciate our own value. We do not find our dignity and worth in how we look, in what we do, or in how much we contribute to the world. Rather, we find our dignity and value simply in the fact that we bear the image of God.

The professor and author J.I. Packer, in his devotional *Your Father Loves You,* wrote: "The image of God in which man was and is made has been variously explained in detail. Although scholars may differ on the nuances of the phrase, there is general agreement that it has to do with dignity, destiny, and freedom. The assertion that man is made in God's image shows each man his true dignity and worth. As God's image-bearer, he merits infinite respect. God's claims on us must be taken with total seriousness. No human being should ever be thought of as simply a cog in a machine, or mere means to an end."[16] This devotional insight from a true sage of the faith really sums it up. As image bearers, we owe one another dignity and respect. This doesn't mean that we can't argue or even dislike each other. But it does mean we must affirm and respect the dignity and worth of every other human being simply because they are image bearers just like us.

As human beings, we have been given explicit gifts because we have been made in the image of God. As such, we have been given unparalleled authority, glory, and dignity. Though we forget and sometimes violate this inalienable truth, we must continue to remind ourselves and each other of it, because in the day we lose hold of it, we will destroy ourselves and the world God has given to us. In Thornton Wilder's classic play *Our Town*, the stage manager says, "We all know that something is eternal. And it ain't houses and it ain't names, and it ain't earth, and it ain't even the stars…everybody knows in their bones that something is eternal, and that something has to do with human beings. All the greatest people ever lived have been telling us that for five thousand years and yet you'd be surprised how people are always losing hold of it. There's something way down deep that's eternal about every human being."[17]

DISCUSSION QUESTIONS

1. What does it mean that we are created in the image of God?

2. How does bearing the image of God affect our value, relationships, and self-image?

3. What does it mean that we are made in the likeness of God?

4. How exactly are we like God and how are we unlike God?

5. Why is it important to recognize the image and likeness of God in ourselves and others?

CHAPTER 3

GOD'S BLUEPRINT FOR OUR FAMILIES

A Christian businessman happily walked into his office one Monday morning and was asked by one of his coworkers how he was feeling that day. "I'm feeling burdened!" he exclaimed. His associate then asked him why he was smiling. The businessman replied, "I'm smiling because I am feeling burdened with the blessings of God!" That's the spirit, isn't it? Imagine how life would be if we all started our week like that, feeling burdened by the immense blessings of God that we carry! That is truly a burden that would be worth carrying.

What does it really feel like to be burdened with God's blessings? Well, ask any human being, because they ought to know. We all ought to know the blessings of God because of the way we were created.

The Bible tells us that when God carefully fashioned people in his image, he endowed them with certain divine responsibilities and heavenly gifts, and these blessings are intended to be received and employed in our daily lives. So then, what exactly are these responsibilities and gifts? In the beginning, God actually blessed people with two responsibilities and with two gifts.

The first of the two responsibilities was procreation. In Genesis 1:28 it says that "God blessed them. And God said to them, 'Be fruitful and multiply and fill the earth.'" To be fruitful and multiply is a direct reference to progeny. The fruit and multiplication refer to having children and having lots of them! God's intention for humanity was to multiply and fill the earth with people.

God blessed the human race with not only the ability to procreate but also the mandate to do so. You'd think that reproduction would be naturally understood and a natural response of men and women toward each other, but apparently Adam and Eve needed a little encouragement that making children was not just acceptable but required! Sometimes, because this was a mandate and not an option, we lose sight of the fact that having children was always intended to be a blessing. Just because something is required doesn't mean it ought to be difficult to fulfill! Having children is and always has been something that God intended to be a blessing for human beings.

I recall having an interesting conversation one day with a close friend a few years ago who wasn't really interested in having kids. Though he was married and his wife didn't agree with him, he was bound and determined to fashion an argument against the mandate to bear children. He talked about overpopulation and unwanted kids, but his most bewildering argument was that he thought having children was the most selfish thing that one could do. When he told me that, I almost fell over in shock. I asked, "How's that?" He said that it was the most selfish thing to do because it's entirely for our own benefit and enjoyment, just like having pets. We love our pets and get a lot of enjoyment from them, but most if not all others don't share our enthusiasm for them. Our pets serve our interests and fill our needs but do not necessarily add anything to the interests and needs of humanity at large. I told him that, interesting as his argument was, it couldn't be reconciled with the original mandate in Genesis that explicitly tells us having children is a blessing from God. If having kids is a blessing, then it cannot be considered a curse. I reminded my friend that one could argue that the act of creating a child is selfish, but the lifelong commitment of raising one is anything but. Every parent who has raised children understands that parenting is incredibly selfless. It can be wonderfully fulfilling, but it can also be absolutely draining. I don't know a parent who hasn't been exhausted and exasperated at times by the unending work of bending and shaping little minds and wills. It is an overwhelming act of love on the part of parents to invest time, energy, and affection into their children so that they can grow up to be adjusted and productive human beings who will in turn contribute to the world.

Having children is a blessing from God to us, and by having them we also become a blessing to the human race. We actually add good to the world when we bear and raise godly children who go out and contribute through their work, gifts, and creativity. We ensure that virtue and truth continue in the world and that the message of the gospel survives to the next generation. Having children is a blessing not just because God said so but because history confirms it. How dark would our world be today if those who have gone before us had refused to bear children and pass on their legacy of faith? Perhaps we ought to consider that we have an obligation, albeit a blessed one, to counterbalance the spread of evil in the world by raising and sending out bold and virtuous witnesses for biblical truth. And if we do not do our part in filling the earth with godly grownups, then we give away the future of this planet to the powers of darkness. Now that would really be selfish.

That being said, it is important to note that even though having children is a blessing, it does not necessarily follow that not having children is a curse. The truth is that many couples are not able to have children even when they want them. As a pastor, I've had the unfortunate privilege of grieving with many young couples who have not been able to conceive or who are not able to carry a baby. Countless couples struggle with this issue and wonder why they are not able to bear children, especially in light of the fact that children are a blessing from God. They feel like not having children is really a curse. But that simply isn't true. The apostle Paul in the New Testament tells us that it is actually a blessing for some not to be married and not to have children because they are able to devote more of themselves to other things, especially in service to God. In Paul's case, he chose to remain single so that he could devote more of his time and energy to spreading the gospel and establishing churches. Biblically, it doesn't make sense to think that not having children is a curse.

In fact, we read throughout Scripture that God has sovereign control over the womb, and he is the one who opens and closes it according to his will. Though we don't understand it from our finite perspective, he does at times close the womb for some women and apparently does it for his own purposes. Those wives who have their wombs closed by God, and their equally exasperated husbands, rarely understand the reasons and often struggle with the timing. I have found that most people who truly desire children will taste that blessing after a season of waiting, but often it seems that God holds out until they learn something he is trying to teach them or do something that he is expecting them to do. In many cases, I have seen couples choose to adopt a child before God opens the womb for bearing their own children. It is really uncanny, but it is true. Time and time again, almost without exception, I have witnessed couples adopt a child after years of trying for their own only to find themselves pregnant shortly thereafter. This process of waiting and obeying is common and serves to prove that not having children is not a curse, but rather a means for God to accomplish his will.

In our case, my wife and I had a long season of heartache

in which God taught us to wait upon him regarding children. We married young and decided to wait ten years before we tried to have a family. Like other young expectant couples, we figured getting pregnant and staying pregnant would be simple. For us, getting pregnant wasn't the problem. Staying pregnant was. We had our first two children, our boys, without issue. But for some reason, God saw fit to close my wife's womb thereafter. We tried and tried to have a third child but struggled through miscarriage after miscarriage. What once seemed simple and easy became complex and anguishing. We tried for three years and lost three babies before God finally gave us our daughter. We were emotionally depleted and ready to give up when God miraculously intervened. It was, without a doubt, the most difficult and draining time of testing in our marriage, but it was also a deep and profound time of learning for us. It was during that period that we learned to fully trust that bearing children is more about accomplishing God's will than ours.

All things considered, the mandate of multiplying is not an absolute promise to all people but rather a general blessing from God to the human race. It is at the same time both a blessing and a responsibility. Now, all the moms who have delivered children know that the actual bearing of children is not the blessing. They might have a different word for it! The act of physically bearing children is not the blessing, especially since God increased the pain involved as a consequence of the fall. The physical pain of delivering a child is not the blessing, the having of children is. I think all new moms can attest to the joy that comes with bearing a child, a joy that far outweighs the pain. The real blessing is bringing children into the world in order to "fill the earth." Apparently, this blessing is so important that God commands it twice, first at creation and later after the flood, so that we might occupy what was then a rather empty earth. The question for us today is, now that the earth is seemingly filled, is bringing more children into the world still really a blessing?

That is a fair question, and it ought to be asked. The answer is that even though filling the earth may no longer be an unfulfilled mandate, having children is certainly still a blessing. We know this because in Psalm 127:3, which was attributed to Solomon, it says, "Behold, children are a heritage from the Lord, the fruit of the womb a reward." According to Solomon, having children is still a heritage and reward from God to mankind. Nothing has changed that tells us that God no longer expects us to exercise and experience the blessing of having kids. Though our reason for bearing children may no longer be to fill an empty planet, it is still to build a godly heritage and receive a divine reward.

The second responsibility God blessed people with is dominion. In Genesis 1:28 we read that "God blessed them. And God said to them, 'Be fruitful and multiply and fill the earth, and subdue it and have dominion over the fish of the sea and over the birds of the heavens and over every living thing that moves on the earth.'" The second half of the mandate to mankind at creation is to subdue and have dominion. These terms in the original Hebrew are royal terms. The language the author uses suggests that this responsibility is kingly in nature. God essentially blessed people with the authority to rule over creation as sovereign and benevolent kings and queens. God has actually delegated his kingship to us in relation to the rest of creation. Now, I prefer to think of it as a vice-kingship or queenship, just so we don't get a false impression of our own importance. God is still the real king over creation. But he has delegated this royal responsibility to us as a blessing to the human race.

This truth ought to be profound for us. Consider the incredible fact that you and I are blessed with a royal responsibility because we are considered kings and queens of all creation! Chances are you have never considered yourself to be royalty. You have probably never thought of yourself as someone who has been crowned by God to rule this world on his behalf. Just knowing that God thinks of us this way ought to change how we see ourselves and other people. It should also affect our sense of purpose and meaning in the world. As God's kings and queens of creation, we have not only the affirmation of God but also his authority to rule the world with and for him. According to God's Word, we have been tapped by the Creator to subdue and have dominion over the whole earth.

To subdue and have dominion over the earth is to have authority over all other created things. The Hebrew word for "subdue" is *kabash*, and it means "to keep under control." Have you ever heard someone say they are going to put the "kabash" on a situation? That ancient Hebrew word means to take control of a situation. It refers to taking charge of something that could easily spin out of control. This refers not only to personal responsibility but hints at governmental responsibility as well. It implies setting up boundaries and making rules that keep creation under control and creatures in line with God's will. Though it doesn't necessarily refer to punishment, it does suggest that enforcement of the boundaries and rules is necessary.

The Hebrew word for "dominion" is *radah*, and it means "to rule over." This term refers to presiding over the affairs of creation and making wise decisions in the interests of God's creation. It implies royal responsibility that should be respected and obeyed by other creatures. Used together, *kabash* and *radah* refer to the general and overarching responsibility of human beings to govern the earth and govern it well. God clearly expects people to rule the earth as he would, which means to do it benevolently. Since God is a benevolent king, he actually expects us to be benevolent kings and queens as well. As we've already seen, this means that dominion is not a divinely sanctioned excuse for us to abuse or exploit the earth. As vice-kings and queens of creation, God wants us to exercise responsible authority and oversight of his creation. By no means does his command give us license to oppress or abuse anything he has created.

God has blessed humanity with the important responsibilities of procreation and dominion. These responsibilities are blessings, but not in a casual sense. A responsibility comes with expectation and accountability. The mandates to be fruitful and multiply and to subdue and have dominion are delegated responsibilities that we must steward and protect.

At creation, God did not just bless us with responsibilities. He also blessed us with gifts. Specifically, God blessed us with two gifts, gifts that do not require our performance but simply our enjoyment. Every human being is entitled to these divine gifts because God gave them to the entire human race. In this way, they really are unassailable gifts, which means that no person or entity ought to take them from us. As such, they are endowed by our Creator and intended for all of humanity. This is where we derive our sense of human rights and personal freedoms as human beings, not just here in America but around the world. It is what drives our belief and commitment to life and liberty for all.

The first of these gifts is provision. In Genesis 1:29, God said, "Behold, I have given you every plant and every tree…you shall have them for food." These gifts to us are the basic and essential provisions we need in order to live full and happy lives. Genesis says that God gave us plants, trees, and their fruit to "have as food," which means that God intended for us to eat the fruits and vegetables that grew on bushes and trees. It is interesting that it was not until after the flood that God later gave animals to humanity as food. Some would argue that because of this, it was not God's intention for us to eat meat from the beginning. They point out that eating meat only came as a substitute after the bulk of our food supply was wiped out during the flood. Though there is merit to this argument, it seems that the debate over this issue is settled in Acts 10 when Jesus speaks to Peter in a vision and tells him that animals are indeed acceptable as food. Some will continue to argue that eating only plants and vegetables is still the biblical ideal, but regardless of one's position regarding what kind of provisions we ought to eat, what we can all agree on is the fact that all these provisions are a gift from God to us!

King David praised the blessing of divine provision for us in Psalm 145:15–16 when he wrote, "The eyes of all [creatures] look to you, and you give them their food in due season. You open your hand; you satisfy the desire of every living thing." David affirmed the blessing of provision, and not just for humanity but for all living creatures. He proclaimed that God not only meets the needs of human beings but also the needs of every living thing. And provision is not just limited to food, but also includes clothing and shelter. In Matthew 6, Jesus told his disciples that our Father in heaven will feed, clothe, and shelter us. Jesus admonished us not even to be anxious about these things because God is always faithful to provide them. Jesus told us that just as the Father feeds the sparrows in their trees and clothes the flowers in the fields, he will do the same for us. In fact, Jesus said that we are "more valuable" to God than the birds of the air or the flowers of the field, and that means he will supply all of our needs better than he does theirs. After all, if God is able to provide for birds and flowers, then he is more than able to provide for his kings and queens.

The second gift from God to mankind is the gift of satisfaction. In Genesis 1:31 we read that "God saw everything that he had made, and behold, it was very good." God intends for us to share his capacity for enjoyment and satisfaction. Scripture says that God actually derived much pleasure from "seeing" everything that he had made. As the Creator, God is creative, and he has made us to be the same way. As image bearers, we are also inclined to create and enjoy the same way that he does. If God derives joy and satisfaction from his creativity, then it makes sense that we would also derive joy and satisfaction from ours. This is because God has blessed us by sharing his capacity for satisfaction with us.

The author J.R.R. Tolkien once described God as the Creator and human beings as his "sub-creators."[18] Likewise, Madeleine L'Engle referred to humans as God's "co-creators,"[19] and Dorothy Sayers called people "little 'c' creators."[20] By referring to mankind in these ways, these authors were getting at the idea that we have not only been delegated God's divine authority to rule but also his divine capacity to enjoy. As creators made in God's image, we also ought to find great pleasure and enjoyment in our work, our hobbies, and our art, just as God does.

Have you ever considered that you were made to enjoy everything that you do? You and I are actually hardwired by God to derive pleasure from the things that we do. That means we are made to delight in what we do for a living and in how we spend our days. The truth is that if your daily routine feels empty and dreary, then something is wrong. Perhaps you've missed the idea that we have been given God's ability to enjoy the things we do. If you don't presently take any pleasure or find any joy in your work, then you probably need to either change your attitude or change your career!

What we see in the creation story is that God was entirely

satisfied by everything that he made. He enjoyed all of the beautiful things and creatures that he had so carefully and thoughtfully fashioned. In fact, this time around God saw everything that he had created and declared it all "very good." What we see here is a special emphasis on the gratification that God takes in his review of creation. Not only is his completed work *tov* or good, it is *very* good. It is almost as if God included that emphatic descriptor to prove a point—and that point is that we were created by a God who really enjoys his work!

If our Creator can find satisfaction, then we can too. This means that our satisfaction in our creativity is a blessing from God to us and something that he wants every person to enjoy. God's satisfaction is supposed to drive our own and provide not just an excuse to enjoy but a veritable reason to do so. *The important conclusion in all this is that life is supposed to be satisfying for us.* It is supposed to provide enjoyment. We ought to stop and "see" everything around us and take special joy in the things we have had a hand in creating.

This relates not just to our professional work but also to our diversions and hobbies. I found out a few years ago that I really enjoy gardening, and since then I have experienced the therapeutic value of working in the yard. Gardening is an artistic outlet for me, and I purposely take time to enjoy the trees, plants, and flowers that I have cared for and sculpted. I often gaze out the window into my backyard and take in how very good everything looks. I know that the enjoyment I gain and the satisfaction I feel is the blessing of God in my life, and that's something we all ought to feel.

Charles Dickens once wrote, "Reflect upon your present blessings, of which everyone has plenty; not upon your past misfortunes of which we all have some."[21] His point is well taken. Every one of us has plenty of blessings to count, and many of those are because of how God created us. His blessings to us are inalienable rights that are intended for every person in every age, and we know this because they are inherent in the creation story. God blessed people with the great responsibilities of procreation and dominion, and he has also blessed them with the great gifts of provision and satisfaction. These blessings are good. In fact, they are *very* good because they come from our Creator. As it says in James 1:17, "Every good gift and every perfect gift is from above, coming down from the Father of lights."

DISCUSSION QUESTIONS

1. What does it mean to be fruitful and multiply? Why did God command it?

2. What does it mean to subdue and have dominion? What does it not mean?

3. What did God provide as food? What are the implications for us?

4. Why did God declare everything to be very good?

5. How are all these responsibilities and gifts blessings?

CHAPTER 4

GOD'S BLUEPRINT FOR OUR TIME

There is an old story about a lumberjack who challenged another to an all-day wood-chopping contest. The challenger worked very hard all day chopping up tree trunks and stopping only for a brief lunch. The other man took several breaks throughout the day and enjoyed a long, leisurely lunch. At the end of the day, the challenger was surprised and exasperated to find that the other man had chopped much more wood than he had. "I don't get it," he exclaimed. "Every time I checked, you were taking a rest, and yet you still chopped more wood than I did!"

"What you failed to notice," said the other man, "is that when I was resting I was sharpening my axe."

Could it be that the key to being more productive is taking regular time for rest? The answer is a resounding yes. As a pastor, I daily encounter people who are exhausted and stressed. According to research, America is the most overworked nation on earth. The work-life balance here in the United States is completely out of whack. The average worker in our country takes less vacation, works longer days, and retires later than the average worker in every other industrialized nation on earth. Chances are that you are working more and resting less now than you used to, and that may be because your life is imbalanced. If you are like the millions of other working Americans, you are probably on the edge of burnout—if you haven't already gone over it.

We operate at a frantic pace in our present world, and we often leave little room in our lives for rest and relaxation. We were not made to operate this way. God didn't intend for us to work all the time, and we are absolutely going to crash and burn if we do. God designed us to take time for rest, to allow ourselves to recoup and recharge. God, in fact, feels so strongly about it that he created a template for work and rest in the creation story. In Genesis, God established a routine that he intends for us to follow.

In the creation story, we read that God worked hard at creating everything for six days, breathing out light and darkness, the planets and stars, the oceans and land, and the plants, animals, and people. And then, he unexpectedly stepped back and rested on the seventh day. How strange to think that the Creator God needed to rest after all that work! He is God, after all, and shouldn't need rest, right? Yet God chose to rest on the seventh day of creation. Why do you think he did it? Was it because he was tired, or did he have something else in mind?

According to the Genesis account, God rested not because he was tired but because he was trying to tell us something. Genesis 2:2 says that, "On the seventh day God finished his work that he had done." The entire first chapter of Genesis describes the incredible work that God accomplished in the short span of just six days. The Hebrew word for "day" is *yom*. There is widespread debate about whether the day refers to a literal twenty-four-hour period of time or to an extended period of time or age, but whatever view one holds to about the length of the creation day, what we can agree on is that it is God who did the creating. Something else we can all agree on is that God rested from his work on the seventh day. Whether the seventh day is a twenty-four-hour period or an age is not really the most important thing. Rather, the more important thing is that the seventh day is distinctly different from the other six! That is, the seventh day of creation is qualitatively distinct and purposefully set apart from the previous six days. So how exactly is the seventh day different? It's different because God rested that day.

In Genesis 2:2 we read that, "On the seventh day God finished his work that he had done, and he rested on the seventh day from all his work that he had done." The Hebrew word for "rest" is *shabbat*, and it means "to cease or desist from activity." Whatever rest is, it is qualitatively different from all the activity that God performed on the previous six days. The Hebrew word for "work" is *melakah*, which refers to an "occupation or profession." So when Scripture says God rested, it means that he ceased from working. That is, he stopped working at his job. Creating was God's chosen profession or occupation, and he deliberately decided to take a break from it. God intentionally diverted his attention away from his job and toward rest. Therefore, the concept of *shabbat* is to cease from labor or from whatever we do during the week to make our living.

Instead of working again on the seventh day, God made the choice to rest. He purposely chose not to do whatever he had been doing during his workweek. God does not get tired, and rest is not something he ever needs, but he still chose to take time to do it. The truth is that God did not rest for his own benefit but for ours! God was modeling what he wanted for us. He was showing us by example that we are created to work, but he was also showing us that we are created to rest. Work is important and should consume the best of our energy, but rest is equally important, and we should also take time for it. This means choosing not to work every day even if we aren't tired. The idea of *shabbat* or "Sabbath" is therefore a divinely sanctioned example that God gave us to follow.

Because God chose to rest on the seventh day, he purposely

consecrated it for humanity. He set the seventh day apart from all the others for a holy purpose. Genesis 2:3 says, "So God blessed the seventh day and made it holy." By making it holy, God turned his example into a command. God gave the command to *shabbat* or rest as one of his Ten Commandments in Exodus 20:8–11, which says, "Remember the Sabbath Day, to keep it holy. Six days you shall labor, and do all your work, but the seventh day is a Sabbath to the Lord your God. On it you shall not do any work...For in six days the Lord made heaven and earth, the sea, and all that is in them, and rested on the seventh day. Therefore the Lord blessed the Sabbath day and made it holy."

It is interesting to note that in the Exodus command, the quote is lifted exactly from Genesis except for one notable difference. In Exodus, the word is changed from "seventh" to "Sabbath." This change is not insignificant, as it makes an important point: the seventh day and the Sabbath day are essentially the same! Because Sunday was regarded as the first day of the week, Saturday was the last and became the official day of rest for God's people, Israel, throughout the Old Testament. Given this parallel, we can see how we ended up with our modern five-day workweek with a two-day weekend. Technically, the Sabbath is Saturday, but there is no longer a technical distinction about the day since Jesus declared in Mark 2:27, "The Sabbath was made for man, not man for the Sabbath. So the Son of Man is lord even of the Sabbath." Because of Jesus's teaching on the subject, we no longer are bound by the law of the Sabbath. And yet, even though we no longer live under the *command* of the Sabbath, we do still live under the *principle* of the Sabbath. God still wants people to get regular rest, though it no longer must be on a specific day or at a specific time. The principle of the Sabbath is that we are designed by God to work for six days, or most of the week, and then rest for one day or at least one part of the week. God hardwired us at creation to rest after work. That is why he consecrated the Sabbath for us, and that is also why he modeled rest.

Perhaps you are one of those people who works too much. You spend a lot of time at the office, and you may not even realize how work has completely overtaken your life. You are coming into work early and leaving late, and it just seems to get earlier and later as time goes by. You might even be working on weekends, going in on Saturdays and Sundays to get caught up on last week's projects or to get a head start on next week's. It probably didn't start this way, but work is swallowing you up and you don't know what to do about it. Maybe you feel like something isn't right in your life, but you are unsure how to change it. After all, you have to get the job done, right? You have to earn that paycheck.

I will never forget the day when I realized that I was working too much. It was a few years ago when I was holding down two jobs. I was working full-time in commercial real estate development and brokerage and working part-time as an associate teaching pastor at my church. Both jobs were demanding, and I felt the pressure to perform. I was going in early and coming home late, and it all culminated when I snuck inside the front door one evening after a long day and slipped into my office to get some more work done. My wife finished preparing dinner and came looking for me. She found me hard at work in my office and asked me to come to dinner. I looked up, removed my glasses, and asked if I could have my dinner in my office. You can imagine how that went over with my wife. It was the straw that broke the camel's back in our home. She growled and stormed off, and it was then that I realized that my life was way out of balance. At that time, no project or paycheck was that important.

God never intended for people to spend themselves slavishly working without any regular time for relaxation and recreation. We were not made to work seven days a week! God himself worked for six days, and he worked quite hard, but he knew the importance of taking a break from that work in order to get refreshed. He considered it important enough to incorporate rest directly into the creation account. Had God not done that and worked for all seven days, we might be prone to think that as image bearers, we would be expected to work just like he did. The problem with this thinking is that though we bear God's image, we are not God. Only Jesus is *the* image of God. We are merely made *in* his image. That means we do not have God's unlimited power, knowledge, and presence, and we are not infinite in strength or eternal in time. Simply put, we are fragile and finite creatures who wouldn't be able to survive that kind of work.

God made human beings, and he made them special. But God did not make us just like him. Only God has the ability to always work and never grow tired. We are different. We do get tired, and we do get sick. We also grow old and die. So unlike God, we must rest. We must take vacations, and we must find time to relax. If we don't, we will break down and fall apart. Because God fully understands our weaknesses as human beings, he intentionally showed us what we are to do, expecting us to follow his lead. This means that we must all find regular time to rest and recuperate. Whether that time to rest is on Saturday or Sunday or any other day, or even if it is spread out over different days and times, is not the important issue. What is important is taking the equivalent of one day out of every seven to cease from doing whatever we do all week.

If you are an accountant, this means you must take one day out of your week not to be an accountant. If you are a teacher, then you must choose one day each week not to teach. The same is true of doctors, plumbers, electricians, and pastors. Whatever it is that we do for a job, we must purposely choose each week not to do it for enough time to catch our breath and recoup our strength. Now, this doesn't mean that we have to sit around and do nothing. It simply means that we need to do something that is different from what we usually do. Perhaps it means playing a game, wrestling with our kids, riding a bike, painting a picture, or tending to our garden. Maybe we can take in a ball game or go see a movie. Whatever we do, we just need to make sure that it is relaxing and refreshing for us.

There is tremendous value in getting away from what we do all week not only to regain our strength but also to increase our productivity. Increasing research suggests a correlation between getting good rest and being more productive in our work. In fact, the evidence shows that while working hours are rising, productivity is actually decreasing in our country. Though people are working more, they are actually producing less. And that is being attributed to the neglect of appropriate rest. Researchers are now suggesting that we take regular intervals and breaks not only on the weekends and on our vacations but throughout our day in order to enhance our effectiveness and increase our productivity.

After all, even Leonardo da Vinci observed the importance of taking time to rest. He famously said, "Every now and then go away, have a little relaxation, for when you come back to your work your judgment will be surer, since to remain constantly at work will cause you to lose power of judgment. Go some distance away, because then the work appears smaller, and more of it can be taken in at a glance, and lack of harmony and proportion is more readily seen."[22]

Unfortunately, many people have misunderstood the principle of the Sabbath and legalistically presumed it means to do nothing that can be considered work of any kind. This has become so silly that some won't permit themselves to pull gray hairs, push buttons on elevators, or even tear toilet paper from rolls. But ceasing from our work means taking a break from our occupation or profession, not from doing anything that makes us sweat or that requires energy. Don't let legalism rob you of the gift God has given to you in Sabbath rest. As Jesus said, "The Sabbath was made for man, not man for the Sabbath" (Mark 2:27). Rest is a gift from God to us that shouldn't be an oppressive burden but a great blessing.

Choosing either to misunderstand the principle of rest or to ignore it altogether comes with a price. Don't pay that price. Not taking the time to regularly rest and recuperate goes against God's design and intention for us, and the consequence is burnout, exhaustion, illness, and even premature death. There are all sorts of news stories and studies put out each year about people who wear themselves out because they fail to take care of their bodies. They work eighty, ninety, even one hundred hours each week and rarely take a day off, and that pace eventually takes its toll. People really do work themselves to death because they neglect to eat properly and exercise, get sufficient sleep each night, or take time out to rest each week. This is a travesty. God intended things to be different for us.

Blaise Pascal once said, "I have discovered that all the unhappiness of men arises from one single fact, that they cannot stay quietly in their own chamber."[23] Pascal rightly attributed much misery in the world to people's inability or unwillingness to follow God's example in the creation account to take time to rest regularly. In the Gospels we see that Jesus challenged his disciples to find times to rest, admonishing them in Mark 6:30 to "Come away by yourselves to a desolate place and rest a while." Even Jesus found the time to get away from his preaching and healing to find rest (Mark 1:35). Jesus knew how important it is for us to find rest, not only for the sake of our bodies, but also for our minds and our hearts. Not only should we take time to recharge our bodies, we should also take time to rest our brains and refill our hearts so we don't burn out.

Jesus felt so strongly about us getting rest that he even promised to give it to those who need it. In Matthew 11:28–29 Jesus said, "Come to me, all who labor and are heavy laden, and I will give you rest. Take my yoke upon you, and learn from me, for I am gentle and lowly of heart, and you will find rest for your souls. For my yoke is easy, and my burden is light." In saying this, Jesus acknowledges that we are too often stressed out and maxed out in this life, and finding rest is something that we actually have to learn how to do. Jesus offers himself up to us as an example to follow. He offers to teach us how to find rest if we just come to him and ask for his help.

The bottom line is that however you choose to rest, do it intentionally and do it regularly. God's example in creation is not a one-time example but a set pattern that is supposed to occur at regular intervals. The key to following God's example is to purposely set aside time to rest on a weekly basis. Understandably, that pattern will be interrupted by life and unexpected events, but strive to maintain some consistency as much as it depends upon you. All sorts of things will vie to throw you off your rhythm, but do your best to reclaim that balance as soon as you can. As most of us know, if we don't schedule things in our calendars, they likely won't happen, so don't be shy about blocking out periods of time each week in your calendar just for you and for the things you enjoy.

Gordon McDonald, in his book *Ordering Your Private World,* put it well: "Does God indeed need to rest? Of course not! But did God choose to rest? Yes. Why? Because God subjected creation to a rhythm of rest and work that He revealed by observing the rhythm Himself, as a precedent for everyone else. In this way, He showed us a key to order in our private worlds."[24] God set a rhythm that he intends for us to follow, and this rhythm is the key not only to our health but also to our happiness in this life.

DISCUSSION QUESTIONS

1. Why did God rest on the seventh day?

2. How is the seventh day different from the first six days?

3. What does the word "rest" mean? Why is it important?

4. What is the principle of the Sabbath? How can we practice it?

5. What will you do to be intentional about taking regular time to rest?

CHAPTER 5

GOD'S BLUEPRINT FOR OUR WORK

Several summers ago, before we had children, my wife, Stephanie, and I decided to take a road trip up the west coast. At the time, we were living in my hometown of Santa Cruz, California, and were preparing to make a move back to Phoenix, Arizona, where I grew up. Before we went back to the desert, we thought it would be fun to drive Highway 1 up the coastline through Northern California, Oregon, and Washington. We decided to use up a couple of weeks and take our time making the drive, stopping along the way to see the rugged beauty of the coast and visit various tourist destinations. Among those destinations was a visit to the famous Butchart Gardens in Victoria, British Columbia.

On our journey through Washington, we stopped off and spent a few days at a comfortable bed-and-breakfast in Port Angeles. One day we took the ferry across the bay to visit the lovely town of Victoria, where we caught a bus to the famous gardens. As we walked through the rows of carefully manicured gardens, we were both struck by the impressive beauty of the place. We so enjoyed our tour of Butchart Gardens that we lamented the fact that we only had the afternoon to spend there. Had we planned better, we would have spent a night or two on the island and taken in more of the wonder of Victoria, but we reluctantly had to return across the bay that evening.

As we later reflected on our day in paradise, we both agreed that it was the highlight of our entire road trip and we would enjoy returning to that location someday. I told my wife that I thought I would entertain changing careers and becoming a gardener if it meant living in a place like that. Though I enjoy being a pastor, I have always thought that being a gardener would actually be more romantic, creative, and interesting. After all, it was the original job that God gave to mankind, and he obviously thought it was a great profession. I guess the idea wasn't without its merit!

In the book of Genesis we see that God created people and put them into a veritable paradise, a garden called Eden. In so doing, God gave them not just the gift of life but also the gift of a calling. He gave them a job. That job was to care for the garden that God had created for them. In the days prior to creating Adam and Eve, God made the earth and filled it with various plants and animals. The Bible says that God planted a vast garden in a place called Eden, and there he grew all kinds of plants and trees. It was here that God placed the first man and woman. It was in this garden that God first gave life and responsibility to human beings.

In Genesis 2:7 we read, "The Lord God formed the man of dust from the ground and breathed into his nostrils the breath of life, and the man became a living creature." It's interesting that God formed man from the "dust from the ground." There is actually a wordplay in the original Hebrew language going on here between *man* and *ground.* The word for man is *adam,* and the word for ground is *adamah*, which suggests a strong connection between people and the ground from which they came. Not only do the two words sound alike, they are intentionally related in order to communicate a verbal picture. You see, the image here is of a potter and his clay, and it points the reader to the relationship between the artist and his work. God, of course, is the artist. People are his art. His palette is the dust and dirt of the ground. In the creation story, God takes mere mud and fashions people from it, which is an amazing creative act in itself. But God doesn't stop there. He brings his artistic clay to life.

Genesis says that God "breathed into his nostrils the breath of life," and the dust came to life. The man then became a living creature, and he was a creature unlike any other. God made man, and then he breathed his own breath into him, making him alive in a way that was completely different from and unmatched by any other thing. Nowhere else in the creation account do we see God breathing this kind of breath into anything else that he made. No, God only gave this particular breath to man, and this difference is an important distinction. Paul in 1 Corinthians 15:39 noted that, "Not all flesh is the same, but there is one kind for humans, another for animals, another for birds, and another for fish." Paul emphasizes the difference between people and all other creatures, and the primary difference is the kind of life that God breathed into them.

The author of Genesis is essentially stressing the fact that mankind has been given a very special gift from God. This gift is the very breath of God. We read that because God breathed his life into man, he became a "living creature." The Hebrew word for "living creature" is the word *nephesh,* which is usually translated as "soul." Because God made people with a soul, they are more than just physical bodies. They are also something spiritual. As human beings, we are physically made of clay, but that is not all that we are. The clay has no life without a soul, and this soul is the gift of life from God. Solomon later told us that we have a body, and it will return to dust, but we are a soul or spirit, and we will return to God after we die. In Ecclesiastes 12:7 he wrote, "The dust returns to the earth as it was, but the spirit returns to God who gave it."

This is critically important because many today think we are only physical beings, people with brains but no soul or spirit. Even many Christians have been misled to believe that there is nothing immaterial about us that lives on after we die. They read and are taught that there is no soul or spirit that exists independently of our body and separates from it upon death. The technical term for this belief is called physicalism or monism, and it has become quite prominent even in some Christian colleges and seminaries. It is the belief that human beings are indivisible physical beings who do not have souls but rather brains that animate our bodies. When our bodies die, then we essentially cease to exist, at least until our bodies are resurrected at the end of the age.

This belief is dangerous because it undermines the creation story and the simple fact that God gave man the gift of life after he made his body. It actually says that man was not made a living creature until after God breathed his breath into him, so his body and God's breath are not the same thing. Just as the body cannot live without the breath, so people cannot live without their soul or spirit. In the gospel of Luke 23:46, for example, just before Jesus gives up his last breath on the cross, he says, "Father, into your hands I commit my spirit," which clearly suggests that the soul or spirit can leave the body just as it comes. This further serves to prove that the soul or the spirit is distinct from the body and that it lives on even after our bodies die.

The great gift that God gave to mankind is the gift of life. God created people, and he created them to live. When he breathed the breath of life into human beings, he intended for them to live and to enjoy the garden he had planted. In Genesis 2:8 we read that "the Lord God planted a garden in Eden, in the east, and there he put the man whom he had formed."

We don't know where exactly this garden was, only that it

was somewhere "in the east." Perhaps God left its location ambiguous so that people would not spend their lives trying to find it. We have a hard enough time as it is not making idols out of ancient artifacts and locations, so it makes sense that God would keep this information vague. I recall visiting Israel a number of years ago and noticing that there is now a church, a temple, or a mosque on just about every biblical site in Palestine. Just about every relic and artifact is carefully protected and venerated, even worshiped, there. One can understand why God would keep treasure hunters and religious zealots from finding every great religious item or site there is. Can you imagine what people would do if they found the Ark of the Covenant or the Holy Grail? God knows that people would not only sell treasures like these but would probably bow down to and worship them.

Despite the mystery of its location, there are some things we do know about Eden. The Hebrew word for "garden" is *gan,* which means "an enclosed and protected area." The etymology of the Hebrew word for *Eden* refers to pleasure and delight. We know that the garden of Eden was a beautiful protected sanctuary that was created by God primarily for the enjoyment of human beings. In the garden, God put "every tree that was pleasant to the sight and good for food." Man had everything he needed in the garden not only to survive but also to thrive. We read that God "put the man" into the garden, which suggests that he placed him there for a divinely intended purpose.

When God created and placed man into the garden, he gave him a twofold purpose, a dual responsibility. The first part of man's responsibility was to work. It says in Genesis 2:15 that "the Lord God took the man and put him in the garden of Eden to work it and keep it." Here we see explicitly what task God gave to Adam. The Hebrew word for "work" is *abad,* and it means "to serve," whereas the Hebrew word for "keep" is *shamar,* and it means "to protect." So, yes, the literal language of Genesis says that man's original task in the garden was to serve and protect it. His responsibility in Eden was to cultivate and guard the garden in which he lived. This involved not just tending to the plants and trees, but actually looking after them. Adam's job was not just to plant and reap, but also to keep watch over the flora under his care, protecting it from harm and destruction. Now, it's unclear what Adam necessarily had to protect the garden from in those early days, but perhaps this responsibility was given for the purpose of setting a precedent for what was to come after the fall, when sin brought corruption not just upon people but also upon the rest of creation.

Whatever the case, there are a couple of substantial implications in this divinely sanctioned duty in the garden. First, the task given to Adam to serve and protect the garden shows that people are entrusted with a responsibility to steward the earth under their care. Today, there is a movement to reclaim our original responsibility, responsibility that has long been diminished and largely ignored. That responsibility is the stewardship of creation. Christians have been slow to adopt creation care, even though Scripture calls us to lead in this regard. It's simply perplexing that we have neglected this duty and even considered it far less important than other forms of stewardship. Thankfully, many are now embracing the original mandate from God not to abuse and destroy the earth but to serve and protect it.

The second implication of our divine duty toward the garden is that it shows us that we are designed by God to work. For many, working is a necessary curse, something we only do because we can't afford not to. If you talk to the average person, you will find that his chief goal in life is probably to retire from work as soon as possible in order to pursue more leisurely things like entertainment and travel. And yet the Bible says nothing of retirement. The idea is really foreign to the Scriptures and actually denies the essence of what God created us to be. By design, we are made to work, and though the nature of that work may change through time and depending on our circumstances, it is not something we are intended to altogether abandon.

Some people misunderstand the nature of work or ignore its intended purpose, which is not to burden us but to empower us. Contrary to popular belief, working is not a result of the fall. Unfortunately, people presume that work is somehow the consequence of sin and contrary to God's original intended design. One of the reasons for this kind of thinking is that God increased Adam's pain and sweat in his work after he sinned, turning his work into hard labor. But God actually did the same thing with Adam's counterpart by increasing Eve's pain in childbirth. And yet her increased pain does not make childbirth itself a curse. In the same way, Adam's consequence of increased pain in labor does not invalidate the blessing of work itself. Hard labor may be a curse for sin, but labor in itself is not.

The truth is that work is a gift from God and not a punishment for sin. Work was never intended to be a curse, but a blessing for human beings from the beginning. It is something that is worthwhile and meaningful, and it is supposed to bring us enjoyment and satisfaction. Many of us can relate to a feeling of completion after a hard day's work. We can appreciate the sense of accomplishment that we have after we do our work and do it well. That is because we are doing exactly what we were created by God to do since the beginning.

Perhaps work for you feels like punishment sometimes. It can be taxing and frustrating, especially when it takes over your life. But God intended work to be a blessing for you. It is something you were created to do, and it is something worthwhile. If you are feeling overloaded by your job and it is not bringing any joy into your life, then the problem could be that you are not appreciating the inherent importance of what you are doing. The Bible tells us that our work matters. In Colossians 3:23, Paul wrote, "Whatever you do, work heartily for the Lord and not for men, knowing that from the Lord you will receive the inheritance as your reward. You are serving the Lord Christ." Paul explicitly told us that our work is our service to Jesus. Our work matters because it honors Jesus, and he rewards it.

In his best-selling book *Good to Great*, Jim Collins closed with these insightful words: "When all the pieces come together, not only does your work move toward greatness, but so does your life. For in the end, it is impossible to have a great life unless it is a meaningful life. And it is very difficult to have a meaningful life without meaningful work. Perhaps, then, you might gain that rare tranquility that comes from knowing that you've had a hand in creating something of intrinsic excellence that makes a contribution. Indeed, you might even gain the deepest of all satisfactions: knowing that your short time here on earth has been well spent and that it mattered."[25]

The second part of man's responsibility in the garden of Eden was to eat. Yes, God not only commanded people to work; he also commanded them to eat. As much as working is a divine mandate, eating is also a mandate from God. Now, this probably comes as a surprise to some people who look at eating as a necessary evil. Those who eat to live and do not live to eat might struggle with this, but the rest of us, who love food, are likely glad to hear it! Food is a blessing from God, and the command to eat it is too. In Genesis 2:16 we read, "The Lord God commanded the man, saying, 'You may surely eat of every tree of the garden, but of the tree of the knowledge of good and evil you shall not eat, for in the day that you eat of it you shall surely die.'"

We often read this Scripture and notice the command about what we're not supposed to eat. What we often overlook is that we are indeed commanded to eat. Scripture says that God "commanded the man" not just *not to* eat from the tree of the knowledge of good and evil, but *to* eat from the other trees. Yes, God commanded Adam to eat. This is something that is strangely familiar in my house, because I have three little children who I often have to command to eat. Like many other kids their age, they like to play with their food at dinner and are easily distracted by other things, so my wife and I regularly find ourselves having to repeatedly remind them to eat their food. We do this because we know they need the nourishment for their bodies.

Perhaps that is the reason why God had to command man to eat his food. As people we often do not know what is best for us, and we easily get distracted from doing the things that are in our best interest. God inserts his divine command right into the creation story to remind us about his intentions for food. The Hebrew word for "command" is *tsavah*, which means "to give orders." God actually gave orders for Adam to eat from the trees in the garden—both for his nourishment and his enjoyment. The command to eat is likely a command not just to feed but also to enjoy! That means the answer to the age-old question, "Do you eat to live or live to eat?" is *yes*.

God expressly commanded that man eat from and enjoy all the fruit of the trees in the garden because that was his intention for people. Earlier in Genesis 2:9 it says that, "Out of the ground the Lord God made to spring up every tree that is pleasant to the sight and good for food." Did you catch that? Yes, it says that God intended food to both be good for food *and* pleasant to the sight. That means food should not only bring us nourishment but should also bring us pleasure. We can conclude that God purposely planted all the trees in the garden of Eden specifically for the nourishment and enjoyment of mankind. The only exception to this was the only tree mankind was forbidden to eat from, the tree of the knowledge of good and evil. This doesn't take away from the fact that God gave every other tree, and a wide variety of fruit, to people for their consumption.

These two responsibilities are not independent of each other. What we see in the Genesis story is that the two actions of working and eating are connected. That really makes sense to us because you really can't have one without the other! As it says in 2 Thessalonians 3:10–12, "Even when we were with you, we would give you this command: If anyone is not willing to work, let him not eat. For we hear that some among you walk in idleness, not busy at work, but busybodies. Now such persons we command and encourage in the Lord Jesus Christ to do their work quietly and to earn their own living." Food is supposed to be the fruit of our labor. If we don't labor, then there is no fruit. Working and eating are interconnected in the creation account because eating is completely dependent upon working. When we work, we are empowered not only to be able to eat but also to be able to enjoy what we eat. That is why work is so integral to fulfilling God's intentions for us on earth.

According to the Bible, God wants us to enjoy our work and to work that we may enjoy our life. Many people miss this critical connection. Perhaps *you've* missed this connection. If you have, then you'll have a hard time appreciating either. God intended for us to work hard and to play hard. But if we don't work hard, then we will not appreciate the value of play. If we never work hard, then we will miss out on the sense of satisfaction and the feeling of accomplishment that is only achieved through meaningful contribution in our work. This obviously goes against the lazy tide of our culture, which prizes the idea of working as little and enjoying as much as possible. The problem with this kind of thinking is that it denies who we really are. Working as little as possible is not how we were created. The truth is that we will be unfulfilled and unhappy if we simply cease to work.

Perhaps this explains why so many wealthy people continue to work even though they have more than enough money to retire. The founders of Facebook are filthy rich and have every reason to sit back and enjoy life rather than keep working. Yet the founders continue to work. Why is that? When asked why he didn't stop working after he became wealthy, Facebook cofounder Dustin Moskovitz said, "If we were just retired, we wouldn't be serving anyone." Likewise, Justin Rosentein said, "When we think of work, we think of work as an act of service, as an act of love for humanity."[26] Both of these men continue to work because they view work as a calling that adds meaning not only to their lives but to the world. They have made the connection between work and enjoyment, and you and I would be wise to do the same.

In an interview published in *Leadership Journal* a few years ago, Pastor Ben Patterson of Westmont College expressed it so well when he said, "I don't believe as some that we should only work to live. I live to work, with this qualifier: God made me to be productive, to do something creative, so I can make a difference in the world. And it's important to have chosen work that matters."[27] As Patterson says, we were designed by God to be productive people. He made us and commanded us from the beginning to work and to enjoy doing it. We are hardwired by God to live and enjoy not only our work but also our food. This is both the gift and the command of God to all of humanity.

DISCUSSION QUESTIONS

1. How did God give life to the body?

2. How did God intend for us to live?

3. Why did God command us to work?

4. Why did God command us to eat?

5. How are working and eating related?

CHAPTER 6

GOD'S BLUEPRINT FOR OUR MARRIAGES

What is marriage? People have suggested all kinds of definitions over the years. Some of them are rather zany and humorous. For example, one person said that marriage is agreeing to spend the rest of your life sleeping in a room that is too warm next to someone who is sleeping in a room that is too cold. Someone else said that marriage is nature's way of keeping people from fighting with strangers, and another said that marriage is like a duet—when one sings the other claps. Whatever your definition, marriage is truly something unique and special. It is a relationship of divine design because God made it and gave it to the world as the most sacred of all relationships.

As time goes by, I find myself ministering to more and more couples who are forgoing marriage because they feel it is outdated and overrated. For many of them, marriage is something that has lost meaning and significance because they don't see it as something sacred. Many have watched their parents go through divorce or stay together in an unhappy marriage, and they have sworn to themselves never to end up in the same predicament. As a result, they have a cynical view of the institution of marriage, so they often end up opting to live together instead.

I've done a lot of premarital counseling through the years, and I have at times conducted classes for engaged couples or those who are seriously considering getting engaged. The last class I led was filled with couples who were living together. It wasn't long ago that living together was a socially unacceptable arrangement even in society, but now it appears to be not only approved in culture but even accepted in the church. I have to admit that I was shocked to find out that every couple was not only living together but that they presumed it was entirely appropriate to do so!

As I have shared God's plan for marriage with couples, they have almost all been dumbfounded by the idea that God would want them to save sex for marriage. Sex was almost automatic for these folks, even for those who considered themselves to be faithful Christians, because they didn't know any different. What I gleaned from these eye-opening interactions is that Christians today are very confused about God's ideal for sex and marriage. Many of them have no idea that God has a plan and intention for marriage and are unaware that following God's plan for marriage is paramount for experiencing his ideal and receiving his blessing in their relationships.

It's possible that you are confused too. This may be the first time you've even considered that God has an ideal plan for marriage that makes it sacred and unlocks his blessing. It might be a foreign idea that God would want more for you than just a mere physical relationship with your partner. The truth is that God wants you to enjoy not just physical intimacy, but emotional and spiritual intimacy with your spouse. But the only way for you to enjoy that level of intimacy and blessing in marriage is if you are willing to follow God's design as he revealed it in the creation story.

The story of marriage begins in the book of Genesis when God first created man and woman. When God first created Adam and Eve, he brought them together in the covenant of marriage, and he did it for some very important reasons. When God initiated marriage, he had specific things in mind for the man and woman. First, God intentionally created man and woman to be different. From the very beginning, God made the first man and woman to be distinct from one other. In Genesis 2:18 we read, "Then the Lord God said, 'It is not good that the man should be alone. I will make a helper fit for him." Notice that when God created Adam, he was the first "not good" in all creation. Now, it is not that Adam was not good; it is that his situation was not. Adam was all alone, and this was something that just was not good. God saw that Adam did not have a partner, so God decided to create one for him.

We read that God made "a helper fit for him." Some older translations translate this as "a help meet for him," which can be a little bit confusing and misleading. The older translations make it sound like the man is somehow superior to the woman. Yet the actual Hebrew language does not suggest anything of the sort. The language does not imply any inferiority for the woman. The Hebrew word for "helper" is *ezer,* and it occurs nineteen times in the Old Testament. Sixteen of those occurrences refer to God himself! In other words, God actually calls himself our "helper" many times throughout the Bible, so there is just no way that the word can denote inferiority. God is inferior to no one and nothing, so the term "helper" is clearly not a slight against the woman in the creation story.

So then, what does it mean to be a helper? It obviously suggests a role of importance, since God himself intends to fill it. To be a helper for someone is to come alongside and provide necessary support. It means to give something that someone else needs or perhaps cannot even provide for him or herself. When God decided to create a helper for Adam, he intended to give him a counterpart, a person who was suitable and able to complete him. The Hebrew word for "suitable" is *kenegdo,* which literally means "facing" or "corresponding to." So when it says that God would make a helper fit or suitable for Adam, it literally means that God wanted to create a person who would correspond to Adam. When the two Hebrew words *ezer* and *kenegdo* are paired together, they say that man and woman are counterparts to one another.

As counterparts, God created man and woman to be fundamentally different. This means it is no coincidence that men and women often feel like they are from different planets. They are! (Whether those planets are Mars and Venus is another story.) The important thing is that men are wired differently than women and women than men. That is no accident. God intended men and women to be opposites in many ways, not so they should live in conflict but so they should live in harmony. Man and woman are different, but different for a purpose—and that purpose is to complete one another.

When God made Adam and Eve, he made them to be complementary. In Genesis 2:20 it says that God made and brought all kinds of animals to the man, "but for Adam there was not found a helper fit for him." Among the creatures God had formed and delivered to the man, there was not one that was a suitable or complementary counterpart for him. None of the animals God had created and provided were sufficient to complete the man. Therefore, it goes on to say, "So the Lord God caused a deep sleep to fall upon the man, and while he slept he took one of his ribs and closed up its place with flesh. And the rib that the Lord God had taken from the man he made into a woman and brought her to the man." Woman was the complement that Adam needed.

The way God fashioned Adam's counterpart is significant because it reveals much about God's intentions for a couple in marriage. God made the woman from a rib he had taken from Adam's side. He fashioned the woman and presented her to Adam as his helper. The question surrounding all this is, why did God choose to use a bone from Adam's side to create her and not just use dust like he did with Adam? After all, God had created every other creature in the creation story up to this point, including Adam, out of dirt. Why use a different method now? The reason seems to be that God had a special relationship in mind for the man and woman, and he illustrated his intentions through his method of creation.

It has been noted by biblical scholars that when God created Eve, he did not choose to take a bone from Adam's head or from his feet but from his side. They agree that this has great significance because it illustrates what it means for a suitable helper to correspond with her mate. The scholar Matthew Henry long ago answered the question perfectly when he wrote in his biblical commentary that "She was not made out of his head to rule over him, nor out of his feet to be trampled by him, but out of his side to be equal with him, under his arm to be protected, and near his heart to be beloved."[28] God did not fashion the woman from the dust like everything else but directly from the man's side in order to communicate the uniqueness of the complementary nature of the marriage relationship.

What makes the man and woman's relationship in marriage so unique is how God intends for them to relate to one another. From the beginning, God intended for the man and woman to be different from each other but also to be equal. We read in Genesis 2:23 that when God brought the woman to Adam, "The man said, 'This at last is bone of my bones and flesh of my flesh; she shall be called Woman, because she was taken out of Man.'" The first thing Adam said when he saw his wife was "at last." Though there is no punctuation in the Hebrew text, we can presume that

Adam was pretty excited when he said this! After sifting through all the animals and finding none that fit him, he finally finds another creature that meets his expectations. You can sense his excitement and relief when he finally meets his bride and exclaims, "At last!" Perhaps the best modern translation of this word would be "Wow!" Of course, that's a very loose interpretation, but you get the point. Adam was stoked about this girl.

Adam was so charged up when he met the woman because he found something in her that he was not able to find in anything else. In Eve, Adam met his match. He found his equal. When Adam first sees her, he says, "This at last is bone of my bones and flesh of my flesh." This is an affirmation of the fact that he recognizes her as his own counterpart. That is, he likes what he sees because she looks a lot like him. She has bones like him and flesh like him, and she probably sounds and acts a lot like him. At the same time, she wasn't exactly like him, and he noticed that too. He noticed that she was physically and perhaps even emotionally a little bit different than he was. Though she was his counterpart and equal, she was also something else that he was not.

What that something was is communicated explicitly in the language of the text, though it is often overlooked or ignored altogether. It's not insignificant that the terms for man and woman are similar but not the same. The Hebrew word for man is *ish,* and the word for woman is *ishah,* and these words literally convey how man and woman are created to fit together. The language is actually quite blunt, as these terms refer to man literally as the "piercer" and woman as the "piercee." Obviously, this implies substantial anatomical differences between man and woman that permit for them to physically connect together, and so this text gives new meaning to the idea that the woman actually completes the man.

Coincidentally, this raw language has a lot to say about the uniqueness and sanctity of the marriage relationship. Since God made man and woman to literally fit together physically, there is inherent and normative evidence in the creation story that God's intentions for marriage are only accomplished between a man and a woman. This means that from the beginning, men and women were made to be physically complementary counterparts who come together in an intimate sexual relationship by God's design. He made each gender to be anatomically different for the purpose of sexual unity, and that means this fit cannot be made between two men or two women. It can only be made between a man and a woman.

Coincidentally, this has much to say to us about our sexual identity. God made men and women different, and we ought to be okay with those differences. There is an enormous amount of pressure in our culture for men to be less manly and for women to be less womanly. In fact, there is a movement in our world today to blend the sexes more and more so that we can hardly tell the difference. They are even making kids toys "gender neutral" these days so that boys and girls can choose their sexual identity rather than be stereotyped by their differences. As we grow up, men are encouraged to find their "feminine side" and women are encouraged to experiment with their "manly tendencies." Both are also encouraged to cross-dress and even consider changing their gender. Furthermore, we are presently experiencing a broad cultural shift toward same-sex marriage and the normalization of homosexuality.

Clearly, gender blending is occurring in our society, and it's never been more difficult for people to see God's design for men and for women through the smokescreen of popular culture. That is why it is so important for us to understand and appreciate God's design and intention for sexual identity and intimacy.

It's critical that we go back to the creation story to identify what God hardwired us to be like as men and women and to access his expectations for unity in marriage.

When we understand and appreciate the original intentions of sexual intimacy, we can see clearly that any aberration from this design is not complementary and cannot create unity. The debate over homosexuality, for example, is best framed in the context of God's original design in the garden of Eden, as it explicitly reveals God's intentions for human sexuality. At creation God made man and woman anatomically different specifically so that they could fit together physically and sexually consummate, and this just cannot be fulfilled by any other combination. To do so is to stray from God's original design and go against the natural order of creation. No matter how much one might want to shift the debate over homosexuality away from the biblical ideal, the scriptural evidence clearly undermines the claims that such behavior is somehow natural.

For this reason, the Bible isolates sexual sin as activity that violates God's original design. Obviously this includes homosexual activity, but it also includes any other sexual activity that is not within the covenant of marriage, including fornication and adultery. God not only intended for man and woman to be equal, but also for them to become one. Genesis 2:24 says, "Therefore a man shall leave his father and his mother and hold fast to his wife, and they shall become one flesh." This is an explicit introduction and clear reference to God's plan for marriage—that man and woman become "one flesh." The Hebrew word for "one" in the verse is *echad*, and it refers to unity and oneness.

When you read the word "one," think of glue. The Hebrew concept of oneness means that separate things are glued together into one. The creation account says that the man shall leave his father and mother and "hold fast" to his wife. That Hebrew word for "hold fast" is *dabak,* and it is often translated as "cleave or be joined." Interestingly, the same word occurs in Job 38:38 and is translated there as "sticks together." In that passage the word *dabak* refers to mud that runs together and forms a clod. When I was a kid growing up in Scottsdale, Arizona, we lived in a new housing development where there was a lot of dirt and mounds on which to play. The neighbor kids would gather outside daily in the vacant lots and have dirt clod wars, which involved creating forts behind each pile of dirt and throwing thick clods of dirt at each other. We would also set up plastic army men on the hills and proceed to knock them down with dirt clods, much like throwing baseballs at milk bottles at the fair. A dirt clod is a hard mass of dirt that is stuck together so much so that it cannot be broken up. It is like the dust has physically been glued or fused together. The dirt in the clod has literally run together and mixed up so much that the individual grains cannot be distinguished at all. There is only one big clod of dirt that looks and feels a lot like a rock. This is the idea that God is getting at in Genesis when he says that man shall leave his father and mother and hold fast or cleave to his wife. This holding fast or cleaving is to be fused together in such a way that the man and woman cannot be distinguished from one another or separated from each other anymore.

This is essentially what Jesus was talking about in Matthew 19:4–6 when he said, "Have you not heard that he who created them from the beginning made them male and female, and said, 'Therefore a man shall leave his father and mother and hold fast to his wife, and they shall become one flesh'? So they are no longer two but one flesh. What therefore God has joined together, let not man separate." Jesus quotes from Genesis and then adds a statement explaining what oneness really means.

He says that in marriage the man and woman are no longer two but one. The husband and wife are glued together in the covenant of marriage, and they cease being two different people because they are now fused into one. This fusion is the blending of two lives physically, emotionally, and spiritually, so much that they become completely integrated. Their lives become so intertwined and mixed together that they no longer can be distinguished or separated.

Jesus also adds that God does the joining together in marriage. He is emphasizing the critical truth that marriage is a sacred union and that God himself presides over it. Marriage is a holy fusion of two people into one by God who facilitates and mediates that oneness. As a pastor, when I marry two people, I explain up front that marriage is not a contract between two people but a covenant among three. It is the covenant made between a husband, a wife, and their God. God is and must be at the center of a marriage, because without his involvement, they only have a contract. Even if our culture calls it marriage, if God does not do the joining, then it is not really marriage. Marriage, by definition, is a sacred covenant of oneness that must be established and upheld by God.

We know that marriage must be both established and upheld by God because Jesus says "what therefore God has joined together, let not man separate." Just as marriage is presided over by God, it is also protected by him. We are warned not to undo what God has done. It may be that we are in fact *unable* to undo what God does. There is some debate among scholars as to whether Jesus meant that people *can't* separate what God has joined or that people *shouldn't* separate what God has joined. Either way, Jesus clearly prohibits people from disrespecting or dismantling the marriage covenant.

Obviously, this is a prohibition against separation and

divorce, which would be the ungluing of two people who have been supernaturally glued together. This is a problem because the language of holding fast or cleaving suggests that the marriage covenant is a permanent promise. When you think of glue, think of permanent glue. We're not talking Elmer's, but Super Glue. The difference between these two is the degree of permanence. Certain glues are stronger than others, and the glue that holds a husband and wife together is stronger than any other kind. That is because the glue comes from God himself. It is supernatural glue. Because a husband is supernaturally glued to his wife in marriage by God, there is no way they can be pulled apart without damaging or even destroying both of them. Consider what would happen if we tried to separate two papers that have been glued together or two bricks that have been cemented. They would both be destroyed. In the same way, two people are so stuck together in the covenant of marriage that they would be totally destroyed if they were to be pulled apart.

Our experience confirms that this is in fact true. Anyone who has been through the experience of divorce or watched someone they love go through it understands the havoc that it wreaks on people's lives, not just on the husband and wife who get divorced but also upon their families and their friends. Divorce destroys relationships. It destroys dreams, and it destroys lives. Those who have been divorced must live with the scars, the guilt, and the pain of that failure, and so must their loved ones. Divorce damages and destroys those who are torn apart and continues to do so over and over again as its repercussions continue to reverberate throughout their lives.

You may have experienced this devastation yourself. If you have been divorced, you know very well how it feels to have the roof cave in on your life. No one starts out thinking that their marriage is not going to last, and nobody expects their vows to ever be undone. And yet divorce happens in this fallen world. Marriages do come apart, and promises are broken. Unfortunately, marital dreams are destroyed. Thankfully, God understands how that feels. Throughout history, God has been divorced by his people when they have broken their covenant with him. The people of Israel whored after other gods constantly, and they often betrayed their promises to be faithful to God. Still, God loved them and never gave up on them. He does the same with the church today when we turn on him by worshiping idols and disobeying his commands.

Divorce is something that God knows too well. Perhaps that is why he hates it so much. In Malachi, God says that he hates divorce because of what it does to relationships, namely to his relationship with us. God despises the destructive force of divorce, and yet he always was willing to forgive and reconcile with his people. The good news is that though divorce has never been God's plan, he has always made provision for healing and forgiveness. So if you have been hurt by divorce, be encouraged that there is hope for you. God can redeem your loss and restore your heart. He can wipe out your sin and give you a fresh start if you will now embrace his plan for marriage.

God's design for marriage from the very beginning has always been that it would be a permanent institution. God desires that husband and wife would experience lasting oneness over a lifetime, not letting anything or anyone tear them apart. Practically, this means that God intended for couples to experience the joy of being faithful to each other, the blessing of giving themselves away in serving one another, and the fulfillment of completing a lifetime commitment to the other. There are so many things we stand to gain in this life through keeping our promises in marriage, and God wants and intends for us to experience all of it.

The truth is that marriage is so much more than just sleeping in a room that is always too warm or too cold. It is more than keeping us from fighting with strangers. And it's not about clapping for the other when they sing. Those are shallow definitions. Likewise, marriage is not about mushy feelings, flowery poetry, and slobbery affection. It is not about romantic songs and feel-good stories. Marriage is about experiencing the deepest and most profound kind of covenant relationship on earth. It is about learning the important lessons in life. And it is about living under the greatest blessings under heaven.

It is as the well-known author Walter Wangerin Jr. wrote: "Marriage is not romanticized in the creation account. Its ideal purpose is not one of sweet feeling, tender words, poetical affections or physical satisfactions—not 'love' as the world defines love in all its nasal songs and its popular shallow stories. Marriage is meant to be flatly practical. One human alone is help-LESS, unable. Marriage makes the job of survival possible. And the fact that a spouse is termed a 'helper' declares marriage was never an end in itself, but a preparation. We've accomplished no great thing, yet, in getting married. Rather, we've established the terms by which we now will go to work."[29]

DISCUSSION QUESTIONS

1. What does the word "helper" mean? What does it not mean?

2. Why did God create woman from man's rib?

3. How do we know that woman is man's counterpart?

4. What does it mean to be "one flesh"?

5. Why is divorce so harmful and destructive?

CHAPTER 7
GOD'S BLUEPRINT FOR OUR FAILURES

Julius Caesar was murdered on March 15, 44 BC. His assassination is arguably the most famous in history because of the bizarre and dramatic way it happened. You see, Caesar was betrayed, and he was betrayed not by an enemy but by his good friend Marcus Junius Brutus, whom he loved and even favored like a son. According to Roman historians, Julius Caesar initially fought back when his assassins attacked him but gave up when he saw his friend Brutus among them. Just before he was struck down, Caesar looked into his friend's eyes with unbelieving shock and sadness and famously said, "Et tu, Brute?" which is Latin for "You too, Brutus?"

This quote has been cited over and over again in celebrated plays, famous films, and even daily conversations as the ultimate expression of the deepest and most heartbreaking kind of betrayal. It has been used to indict all kinds of treasonous turncoats through the ages who have committed the most heinous offenses, and it has come to symbolize the very worst in humanity. I think most people would agree that betrayal is just about the worst thing that one person can do to another, especially to a trusted friend or family member. I suppose one could argue that murder is worse, but I'm not sure that it really is. I think betrayal is just about as bad as murder, and it may actually be just another form of it. Betrayal is heartbreaking and devastating, and it has its origins in the very beginning of our world.

The story of betrayal begins in the garden. It starts in a place that was a sanctuary of blessing and beauty, in a place where the first two people lived in perfect harmony with God and with each other. Everything was right and good in the garden. That is, until that day—the day when that harmony was disturbed and destroyed, the day when it was ruined by betrayal of the worst kind. The man and the woman had been living in that garden, enjoying perfection and intimacy, when the serpent slithered into the picture, tempting them and misleading them and starting them down the dark road of betrayal. What happened is called "the fall" because paradise was lost on that day. Mankind stabbed God in the back when it happened, and nothing would ever be the same.

Genesis 3:1 tells us, "Now the serpent was more crafty than any other beast of the field that the Lord God had made. He said to the woman, 'Did God actually say, "You shall not eat of any tree in the garden?"'" The whole day started with a serpent, a snake that was more clever and devious than any other animal. The Scriptures tell us this serpent was none other than Satan himself, taking the form of a conniving creature. In Revelation 12:9 he is identified as "that ancient serpent, who is called the devil and Satan." He was there in the garden that day, and Scripture says that he was crafty. The Hebrew word for "crafty" is *arum,* and it means to be "shrewd or cunning." It suggests that the serpent was skilled to mislead and confuse, and deceive he did.

Satan deceived the woman by distorting the command of God. The snake contorted God's command to eat by putting his own wily spin on it. He subtly changed God's words to appear harsh and restrictive. He plainly ignored God's generous provision and emphasized his only prohibition. Remember that God gave the man and woman much freedom to eat from any tree in the garden and only forbade them eating from one. And yet Satan reminded them of that one. For us, this would be like telling a child, "Your parents don't love you because they don't let you play in traffic." We give our children lots of freedom, but we also give them boundaries because we love them, not because we want to deny them freedom. Of course, they don't understand that. They're prone to only see the things they don't have, and sometimes others see it for them.

What Satan failed to disclose when he deceived the woman was that God's only boundary was actually for her benefit. In Genesis 2:17 God told them, "Of the tree of the knowledge of good and evil you shall not eat, for in the day that you eat of it, you shall surely die." God forewarned them that eating from that particular tree would end up killing them. He did not forbid them from eating just because he wanted to control them. No, God forbade them from eating because he wanted to protect them. God did not want them to die. Satan conveniently left that part out. Instead, he tempted the woman, and he lied to her.

In Genesis 3:2–4 it says that, "The woman said to the serpent, 'We may eat of the fruit of the trees in the garden, but God said, "You shall not eat of the fruit of the tree that is in the midst of the garden, neither shall you touch it, lest you die."' But the serpent said to the woman, 'You will not surely die.'" The woman spoke to the snake and answered his treasonous question, and her response was both to minimize the threat and to twist God's words. Notice that she adds a prohibition to God's command, inserting "Neither shall you touch it" to God's prohibition. It is important to note that God never said they couldn't touch the fruit. God never told them that.

As a parent, I can't count the number of times my kids have changed my words. When they disobey, I will often ask them to repeat what I told them to do, and it is amazing how differently they remember what I said. My kids not only forget what I told them but even seem to make up new things! My middle child, Christian, who is five years old, is one of those random kids who will say things that have absolutely nothing to do with anything I just mentioned. For example, I may tell him to clean up his room, and he will either ignore me or pretend not to hear me. I will then tell him to repeat back to me what I said, and he will say something like, "We should play games and have fun." Or he'll repeat back something similar, like, "You said to pick up our toys…but that we should play for a few more minutes first." Um, that's not what I said exactly. Even as cute little children, my kids are still sinfully inclined to twist or tweak my words.

The fact that the woman so easily and willingly twisted God's command is solid evidence that Satan was able to effectively mislead and confuse her. Her confusion is apparent in the fact that she responded by telling the serpent a half-truth about God when he asked her the question. We all know that a half-truth is not really the truth. It is a lie. This is essentially what Satan was after, since he himself is a liar by nature. Jesus described the nature of the devil in John 8:44 when he said, "You are of your father the devil, and your will is to do your father's desires. He was a murderer from the beginning, and has nothing to do with the truth, because there is no truth in him. When he lies, he speaks out of his own character, for he is a liar and the father of lies."

The fact that Satan followed up his deceptive question with a lie is no surprise. As it says, "The serpent said to the woman, 'You will not surely die.'" This is not even a half-truth. It is a complete lie. God clearly told the man and woman that if they ate of the fruit, they would indeed die. Satan's explicit denial is a flat-out contradiction and blatant rejection of God's command. In doing this, he not only betrayed the man and woman, he also betrayed God. Satan betrayed God by deceiving the woman he had created and by lying about his promises. In so doing, Satan disrupted and destroyed the fellowship between God and people. He started the chain of betrayal that began with him but ends with us.

God was betrayed by Satan, by his deception, and by his lies. But God was also betrayed by people. He was betrayed by their pride and by their disobedience. In Genesis 3:5, Satan says, "For God knows that when you eat of it your eyes will be opened, and you will be like God, knowing good and evil." We read that Satan lured the woman into sin by tempting her. But what exactly did Satan tempt her with? Scripture says that he tempted the woman with "knowledge." The serpent claimed that she would become "like God, knowing good and evil." The Hebrew word for knowing is *yada*, and it means "to perceive or recognize." This knowledge is not a general reference to knowing information or gathering facts but to discerning the difference between what is good and evil, right and wrong.

Up until this point in time, it appears that the man and woman had been living in blissful ignorance. They were naively enjoying the pleasures and blessings of life in the sanctuary that God had given them, blissfully unaware of the existence of evil and wrong. They only knew God and the good things he had revealed to them. They had no perception of evil and all the pain, suffering, and loss that came with it. The man and woman had no idea what life would be like if they knew about evil. They could not fathom how the world would change once they did. It never occurred to them to stop and think about it. They jumped at the opportunity to "be like God." It was just too much to resist.

It is interesting to note that Satan tried to do the very same thing with Jesus when he was being tempted in the wilderness for forty days. In Matthew 4:1–3 we read that "Jesus was led up by the Spirit into the wilderness to be tempted by the devil. And after fasting for forty days and forty nights, he was hungry. And the tempter came." The tempter, naturally, was Satan, who tried to lure Jesus into sin just as he did the woman in Genesis. He tried to tempt Jesus with possessions, with power, and with pleasure. He offered him the opportunity to "be like God" too, but Jesus didn't fall for it. Where the woman failed, Jesus succeeded. As it says in Hebrews 4:15, "We do not have a high priest who is unable to sympathize with our weaknesses, but one who in every respect has been tempted as we are, yet without sin."

The woman fell for Satan's tricks, not because she was dumb but because she was prideful. It was her pride that led her into sin. She longed to have something that did not rightfully belong to her. She wanted to be equal with God. This is the gravest of all sins because it is the very sin that ruined Satan long before our world was created. Pride is the original sin because it is the very thing that upended heaven and led to the casting down of Satan and his angels.

Scripture tells us that before he was Satan, the enemy was a beautiful and beloved angel named Lucifer. In Ezekiel 28 we get a glimpse into the story and the reason Lucifer fell from heaven. It says in Ezekiel 28:12–17, "You were the signet of perfection, full of wisdom and perfect in beauty. You were in Eden, the garden of God…You were an anointed guardian cherub. I placed you; you were on the holy mountain of God; in the midst of the stones of fire you walked. You were blameless in your ways from the day you were created, till unrighteousness was found in you…Your heart was proud because of your beauty;

you corrupted your wisdom for the sake of your splendor. I cast you to the ground; I exposed you before kings, to feast their eyes on you." The prophet tells us that Lucifer was cast out of heaven because of his pride. Pride is the original sin, and it is the very thing that led to the woman's betrayal.

In Genesis 3:6 we are told, "So when the woman saw that the tree was good for food, and that it was a delight to the eyes, and that the tree was to be desired to make one wise, she took of its fruit and ate, and she also gave some to her husband who was with her, and he ate." I noticed a bumper sticker on a car the other day which read, "Lead me not into temptation, I can find the way myself." It's true that people don't need any help to fall into temptation. The Scriptures tell us that we are predisposed toward temptation because we have always struggled with personal pride. It doesn't take much—sometimes just a tempter to come along and draw it out.

In the case of the woman in the garden, she simply looked and saw that the fruit was "good for food, a delight to the eyes and desired to make one wise." All Satan had to do was place temptation right in front of her in order for her to start lusting for it. And lust she did.

Throughout the Bible we find that there are essentially three categories of lustful temptation that Satan floats under our noses. They are possessions, pleasure, and power. John describes these in 1 John 2:16–17 where he says, "All that is in the world—the desires of the flesh and the desires of the eyes and pride in possessions—is not from the Father but is from the world. And the world is passing away along with its desires, but whoever does the will of God abides forever."

It's interesting to see that Satan did not strong-arm the woman into sinning. In fact, he never seems to have to do that. He only needed to set the temptation in front of her and perhaps package it in a form that appealed to her. Whether he put an extra sheen on the fruit to make it look more ripe or whether he offered it up when her stomach happened to be growling, we don't know. All we know is that Satan got her to look at it in such a way that she wanted it. The truth is that Satan finds all sorts of devilishly creative ways to package up temptations for us so that we will be more likely to fall for them. He knows our weaknesses and our appetites, and all he has to do is put the things we lust for within reach for us to go after them.

Satan uses the same ploys to tempt us still today. He subtly floats the things we're weak for in front of us, drawing our eyes so that we will crave what is being offered. It may be pornography, it may be money, it may be alcohol, it may even be food. I've counseled men whose sex addiction started with a simple pop-up on a website. All Satan had to do was put a link on a web page they visited, and the next thing they knew they were hooked on hard-core pornography and visiting prostitutes. It always starts somewhere. For those who lust for alcohol or drugs, it usually started with a small sip of wine or a slight puff on a cigarette. Those who struggle with gluttony can often trace it back to a soothing chocolate truffle after a hard day. The devil is very clever, and he knows our desires. He likes to exploit them by sending temptation our way in nondescript ways, even shrouding them in seemingly harmless chat rooms, seating them next to us on bar stools, placing them at the bottom of bottles or on top of dessert trays.

When the woman "saw" the temptation in front of her, she couldn't stop herself from reaching out and taking it. The Hebrew word for "saw" is *raah,* and it is eerily similar to the Hebrew word for "know," *yada. Raah* also means "to perceive or recognize," so it suggests that when the woman saw, she sinned before she even ate the fruit. She sinned when she desired it—

it was her lustful intent that was sinful. Later Jesus would explain that lust is a sin of the heart even before it becomes an action. In Matthew 5:28 Jesus said, "I say to you that everyone who looks at a woman with lustful intent has already committed adultery in his heart." Eve's sin started in her heart even before it became an act.

Unfortunately, Eve brought her husband into her sin when she offered him fruit too. "She gave some to her husband who was with her, and he ate." The only difference between his sin and hers was that Adam knowingly sinned. Whereas the woman was deceived into sin, Adam willingly did it! The entire time the serpent was tempting Eve and lying to her, Adam was standing right next to her, and he didn't say a thing. The text says nothing about him being deceived, so he knew what was happening all along. In fact, the apostle Paul explicitly says in 1 Timothy 2:14 that Adam was not deceived like the woman was. Whether he was too passive or weak to say something or whether he was simply tempted by the same lusts as the woman, we can't be sure. It is possible that it was both. Either way, Adam failed in his role as a husband to protect and lead his wife.

Instead of interceding to defend her from Satan's ploy, Adam stood idly by and gave in himself. His failure as the husband was actually worse than hers as the wife because his was intentional. Clearly, God held him responsible for their sin, because after the fall God came looking for them in the garden and called for Adam, not Eve. In Genesis 3:9 we read that, "The Lord God called to the man and said to him, 'Where are you?'" This is the consummate question, because it not only shows us which one of them God holds responsible for their betrayal, but it also illustrates for us the sinfulness of men's passivity. Husbands and fathers are notorious for abandoning their responsibilities to their families. Fathers are absent from their kids and husbands are distant from their wives because they have always been inclined to stand by.

Husbands and fathers are not supposed to stand around and let their wives and families fall apart. They were made by God to lead their homes toward godliness and provide spiritual direction and care to their wives and children. God intended for Adam and his descendants to love and lead their wives by providing for and protecting them. This is made clear in Ephesians 5, where Paul roots the role of the husband in the Genesis story. He writes in Ephesians 5:25–31, "Husbands, love your wives, as Christ loved the church and gave himself up for her, that he might sanctify her, having cleansed her by the washing of water with the word, so that he might present the church to himself in splendor, without spot or wrinkle or any such thing, that she might be holy and without blemish. In the same way husbands should love their wives as their own bodies. He who loves his wife loves himself. For no one ever hated his own flesh, but nourishes and cherishes it, just as Christ does the church, because we are members of his body. 'Therefore a man shall leave his father and mother and hold fast to his wife, and the two shall become one flesh.'"

For Paul, the foundation for how a man ought to lead in his marriage and family is clearly set in the creation story. God specifically made man to "nourish and cherish" his wife from the beginning. A husband nourishes and cherishes his wife by providing for and protecting her. In Adam's case, he failed as both provider and protector. When his wife sinned, Adam let her down in a profound way, and he knew it. The evidence that he knew he had failed is his awareness of guilt and shame. Because of their sin, it says in Genesis 3:7, "The eyes of both were opened, and they knew that they were naked. And they sewed fig leaves together and made themselves loincloths." The fact that they became self-conscious and embarrassed shows that Adam and his wife knew they had sinned and betrayed God.

Most of us know when we've slipped into sinful patterns. Though we tend to make excuses or try not to notice what's happening, the reality is that we know inside when a simple desire has become full-blown debauchery. The Bible says in the book of Romans that we are all without excuses because God has given us all an intuitive awareness of our sin. This intuition is called conscience. In Romans 2:15–16 Paul wrote, "[Gentiles] show that the work of the law is written on their hearts, while their conscience also bears witness, and their conflicting thoughts accuse or even excuse them on that day when, according to my gospel, God judges the secrets of men in Christ Jesus." According to Paul, we all have a conscience that God has given us that causes dissonance in our spirit when we are in sin. In other words, we all know when we're violating God's command because our conscience tells us.

I've come to appreciate that my conscience is really the voice of the Holy Spirit who tells me when sin has invaded my life. Because the Spirit of God dwells within us as Christians, we ought to be able to hear his voice when he calls us out. The Bible describes the voice of the Holy Spirit as bringing sin to our attention so that we will feel conviction. Conviction is the work of God in our life when he shows us how we've gone astray. He reveals to us the ugliness and the darkness of the sin that takes over in our life.

Perhaps you have felt the conviction of God's Spirit in your life. You'll know the voice of God when you hear it because it is an unmistakable feeling in your gut that you've let him down. That's called conviction, and it's a good thing. It wakes us up to our sinfulness and keeps our own heart soft before God. Guilt and conviction are not the same thing. Guilt comes from man, and guilt only creates a feeling of shame. It doesn't motivate us to make changes. Conviction, on the other hand, comes from the Holy Spirit, and it inspires us to deal with our sin because it impedes our relationship with him and often comes with consequences.

The consequences for Adam's and his wife's sinfulness were immense because their sin brought corruption and judgment upon the world and all of their descendants. For this reason, their betrayal goes down in history as the most monumental sin of all time. This could have spelled the end for all hope and for all happiness. But thankfully, it didn't. The fall was a terrible day, but at the same time, it was a blessed day. How so? John Milton in his *Paradise Lost* calls the original sin in the garden a "felix culpa," which is the Latin phrase for "fortunate fall."[30] According to Milton, those who have lost something of great value can appreciate it more fully when they have found it again. For Adam and Eve, as well as for all those who come after them, there is always the opportunity to regain what was lost.

The Bible tells us that we can recover what was lost in the garden through faith in the new Adam, who is Jesus Christ. The Scriptures say that his forgiving work on the cross actually undoes Adam's betrayal in the garden, and that paradise lost can become paradise regained for all who believe in him. As it says in Romans 5:12, 18, "Therefore just as sin came into the world through one man, and death through sin, and so death spread to all men because all sinned [betrayed]…Therefore, as one trespass led to condemnation for all men, so one act of righteousness leads to justification and life for all men."

DISCUSSION QUESTIONS

1. Who is the serpent? How do we know?

2. How did the serpent deceive the woman?

3. What lie did the serpent tell her?

4. What did Satan use to tempt her?

5. How did the woman sin? How did her husband sin?

CHAPTER 8

GOD'S BLUEPRINT FOR OUR EXCUSES

The famous basketball coach Frank Layden once confronted one of his players who was underperforming and said to him, "Son, what is it with you? Is it ignorance or is it apathy?" To which the player replied, "Coach, I don't know and I don't care."[31] The quote is funny, but it's also sort of sad. It conjures mixed feelings because it confirms what we all probably know is true about us. Deep down, we know that we are creatures who tend to make a lot of excuses for ourselves. We are quick to avoid blame and even deflect it somewhere else. It's almost automatic. We hate taking the blame for anything that we do wrong, and this tendency goes back all the way to the very beginning. In fact, it goes all the way back to the garden.

I think counselors call this blame shifting. It's a clever term to describe the oldest self-defense tactic known to mankind. Blame shifting is the tactic of avoiding taking responsibility for our actions. It is the oldest tactic of avoidance because it originates in the garden with Adam and Eve, who were the first, but certainly not the last, to blame everyone but themselves for their sin. As we've already learned, Satan in the form of a serpent tempted and deceived the woman into sin, and she in turn facilitated her husband's sin when she gave him the fruit to eat. When this happened, God came looking for them and confronted them. And what did they do? They blamed others, of course. They shifted the blame to God, to Satan, and to each other.

As I mentioned in the previous chapter, we all have an internal sense of our sin because of our conscience; the challenge for us is whether we are willing to admit it. Our tendency is to make excuses for ourselves and blame others for our sins. Rather than accept blame for our drinking, we blame the problem on the devil for creating all of the problems in our lives. We pin our anger issues on our parents because they didn't really love us. And we blame our spouses for our infidelities because they failed to show us any respect or affection. But all of this blame shifting only gets us caught in a vicious, endless cycle that never gets resolved. We never end up dealing with our sin because we don't place the blame where it belongs—at our own feet.

In Genesis 3:8–9, after Adam and Eve had tried to pin the blame for their sin on each other, on the snake, and even on God himself, it says that "They heard the sound of the Lord God walking in the garden in the cool of the day, and the man and his wife hid themselves from the presence of the Lord God among the trees in the garden. But the Lord God called to the man and said to him, 'Where are you?'" We read that after they had sinned, God came looking for them. Knowing that God was in hot pursuit, they tried to hide themselves somewhere among the trees. That did not work out so well. I mean, did they really think they could hide from the God of the universe? It seems plain silly for them to try to hide out from the all-knowing Creator, and yet it did not stop them from trying!

We tend to do the very same thing. We try to hide from God because of our sin. We sneak into dark places where we think we can't be seen, but God always find us. We might try to hide out from God by going places we think he doesn't go. We may sneak into a bar and grab a table in a dimly lit corner where we can drink our sorrows away because surely God doesn't go to bars, right? Or we may disappear into our bedroom and seek solace in that illicit chat room because certainly God is not on the Internet, right? Wrong.

It doesn't matter where we try to hide or how hard we work to ignore God's call. We can run to the end of the earth and we can hide in the deepest cave, but God always knows where we are. You might be trying to hide from God. There may be sin in your life that you've been trying to escape, but you will find that there is nowhere you can go where God cannot find you. He knows where you are, and he knows what you've done. So you might as well give yourself up. The God of creation knows you and pursues you, and he will go to great lengths to reach you.

The truth is that there is nowhere we can go to hide from God. There is no valley too deep, no mountain too high, and no land too far for God to find us. As it says in Psalm 139:7–10, "Where shall I go from your Spirit? Or where shall I flee from your presence? If I ascend to heaven, you are there! If I make my bed in Sheol, you are there! If I take the wings of the morning, and dwell in the uttermost parts of the sea, even there your hand shall lead me, and your right hand shall hold me." David understood there was no place we can hide from God where he cannot find us. The reality for us, as it was in the garden, is that God knows where we are at all times. There is no place we can go where he cannot reach us.

God knew where Adam and his wife were hiding. The branches of the trees were not enough to shield them from his eyes. That is why it says God "called to the man." The Hebrew word for "called" is *qara*, which means "to summon." This is important because it means God's summoning of Adam was a command to appear. When you and I receive a jury summons in the mail, we are required to appear in court unless we are formally excused. In the same way, God literally summoned Adam and required him to come out from where he was hiding. God wasn't so much calling *to* the man as he was calling *out* the man.

God held the man responsible for what happened in the garden. Even though both of them had sinned, God came after Adam first because he was held accountable for their betrayal. Remember that the difference between his sin and his wife's sin is that she was deceived into sinning while he knowingly chose to sin. Eve was deluded into eating the fruit, but Adam ate it willingly. He could and should have intervened to protect and correct Eve when she was telling the half-truth, and he could have and should have confronted Satan when he lied to her, but he didn't! No, Adam stood idly by and watched it all unfold. Genesis 3:6 tells us that "She took of its fruit and ate, and she also gave some to her husband who was with her and he ate." Adam was there with her the whole time and didn't do a thing. That is why God came and called him out.

Husbands have an incredible responsibility toward their wives and families. In Ephesians 5:25, Paul admonishes husbands to "Love your wives, as Christ loved the church and gave himself up for her." He tells fathers in Ephesians 6:4, "Do not provoke your children to anger, but bring them up in the discipline and instruction of the Lord." Paul clearly challenges husbands and fathers to look after their wives and children, loving them, sacrificing for them, and bringing them up in the things of God. In the same context, Paul roots all of these responsibilities directly within the creation story, which confirms that God's design in Genesis is not just an ideal for men but a divinely ordained responsibility.

Adam did not do these things. He shirked his manly responsibilities. God confronted Adam for his sin because it affected not just him but those around him too. It is important for men to realize that their decisions deeply affect others, especially those closest to them. Their choice to live selfishly or passively comes at a steep cost, and that cost is well illustrated here in the creation story. Adam failed his family, and that is why God came after him. If we fail our families, we can presume that God will come after us too, not to punish us but to call us out for not being the men we were created to be.

God confronted Adam for failing as a husband, but God did not let Eve off the hook for her sin either. In Genesis 3:13 it says that "The Lord God said to the woman, 'What is this that you have done?'" In 1 Timothy 2:13, we are told that "Adam was formed first, then Eve; and Adam was not deceived, but the woman was deceived and became a transgressor." Eve's sin was the fact that she was deceived. Her mistake was falling into deception, and the reason it happened was that she failed to fulfill her responsibility as a wife.

In Ephesians 5:22–24, Paul tells us what the wife's responsibility to her husband is, writing that wives should "Submit to your own husbands, as to the Lord. For the husband is head of the wife even as Christ is the head of the church, his body, and is himself its Savior. Now as the church submits to Christ, so also wives should submit in everything to their husbands." This command is also rooted in the creation order, so Eve's responsibility was to submit to or support her husband. Practically, this means that she should have consulted with Adam before taking the fruit and eating it. Had she sought the counsel of her husband and his approval beforehand, she might not have fallen for the lies told by the serpent.

The lesson here is that wives were created by God to support and respect their husbands. Supporting and respecting a husband includes seeking his guidance and counsel as protector of the family and soliciting his input and approval as the leader of the home. When the wife fails to consult with the provider and leader of their family in critical matters and important decisions, especially those of a spiritual nature, she has the potential to be deceived and manipulated. This does not mean that women are somehow naturally more gullible than men but simply that wives are more vulnerable and susceptible to the dangers and deceptions of the Evil One without the protection and guidance of their husbands.

Because she failed to consult her husband and succumbed to deception, God scolded Eve. He essentially asked her, "What have you done?" God is not really asking because he wants to find out. He is asking because he already knows! Have you noticed that this is the kind of question we tend to ask when we already know what someone has done? I have asked this question many times in frustration, as more of an exclamation than a question. When my kids break something, and I ask them what happened, it is quite obvious what occurred—I just want to hear them own it. I expect to hear them say it. This is what God was doing with Eve. He wanted to hear her confess what she had done.

God asked the woman about what she had done in order to expose her sin. In this way, God was acting like a concerned parent trying to elicit a confession from his wayward child. This is critically important because it shows us that God is just and that he does not unfairly or prematurely dole out judgment upon us. Notice that God did not act out in anger over her sin and pass out a sentence flippantly or dispassionately. God is a loving and patient parent who carefully works with his kids to help them come to grips with their sin. What we see and should learn from the creation story is that God is a loving parent to us, one who cares enough to confront us when we act like rebellious children and betray him.

I will never forget the time when I screwed up as a neophyte sixteen-year-old driver who had just gotten his license. I was on my way to pick up my father from work. I was driving his car, and I got pulled over for speeding in a residential zone. The officer gave me a ticket, and it made me pretty upset. I dreaded what my father might say when I pulled up to his workplace. I imagined all kinds of horrible things and prepared myself for the worst. But my dad wasn't angry. He didn't yell at me. He didn't even give me the stink eye. Rather, he simply asked me what happened and told me that it was okay. He affirmed his love for me and told me there was grace for my mistake.

You may not have been blessed with a loving parent who dealt graciously with your mistakes. You may have had a mom or dad who always overreacted when you spilled your milk or broke your toy. Many parents fail their kids by dealing too harshly with their mistakes, often criticizing or belittling them for their blunders. So many people today have a hard time appreciating God's kindness and mercy as our heavenly Father because their human father let them down so much. It can be difficult to understand that God deals lovingly and graciously with his children in a way that isn't destructive. He never makes us feel guilty, and he never shames us even when we probably deserve it.

When God's first children sinned, he didn't fly into a rage and rashly punish them for their rebellion. Instead, he lovingly and carefully confronted them in an effort to get them to own their sin and confess it. However, they did not respond well to God's gracious accountability. Instead, we read that they shifted the blame to others. First Adam blamed God, and then he blamed his wife. To make matters worse, Eve blamed Satan for her sin. Instead of taking responsibility, they deflected it like immature children trying to get away with their betrayal.

When God confronted Adam, he turned the blame right back on God. Genesis 3:9–12 says, "The Lord God called to the man and said to him, 'Where are you?' and he said, 'I heard the sound of you in the garden, and I was afraid, because I was naked, and I hid myself.' He said, 'Who told you that you were naked? Have you eaten of the tree of which I commanded you not to eat?' The man said, 'The woman whom you gave to be with me, she gave me fruit of the tree, and I ate." Did you catch that? Adam said it was the woman whom "you" gave me. In other words, it is God's fault because he gave Adam the woman.

It was Philo of Alexandria who wrote, "When the mind has sinned and removed itself far from virtue, it lays blame on divine causes."[32] Because Adam's mind was hampered by sin, he did exactly what depraved men do. He blamed it on God. Instead of accepting responsibility for his failure to protect his wife and his own soul, he deflected blame toward God. And then he went even further. He also blamed his wife! After trying to pin the blame on God, he next tried to shift it onto her, saying, "She gave me the fruit of the tree, and I ate."

The truth is, Adam should have blamed himself. The Scriptures tell us that we cannot blame God for our own sinfulness. James 1:13 reads, "Let no one say when he is tempted, 'I am being tempted by God,' for God cannot be tempted with evil, and he himself tempts no one." Likewise, the Scriptures tell us that we cannot blame others for our sin. Galatians 6:4–5 says, "Let each one test his own work, and then his reason to boast will be in himself alone and not in his neighbor. For each will have to bear his own load." We cannot shift the blame for our own sins onto others. We cannot blame God. We cannot blame our spouse. We cannot blame our kids, our family, our friends, or anyone else for that matter. No, we can only blame ourselves for our sins.

Unfortunately, Eve did not do any better. God scolded her too, but she tried the same failed defensive strategy as Adam.

Genesis 3:13 says, "Then the Lord God said to the woman, 'What is this that you have done?' The woman said, 'The serpent deceived me, and I ate.'" Whereas Adam blamed God and his wife, Eve actually blamed the snake! She said her sin was the serpent's fault because he deceived her. Eve pointed the finger at Satan and tried to indict him for her sin, but it didn't change the fact that she had done the sinning.

Despite their failed attempts to shift blame, it is interesting to note that both Adam and Eve did end up admitting that they ate the fruit. This is an admission of the fact that they did indeed sin. After all, the snake did not make Eve eat the fruit, and Eve didn't make her husband eat it. Neither of them was held down and force-fed. They did it by their own volitional choice. Both of them admittedly said, "I ate it." They realized they were not going to get away with their sin. They could not pull the wool over God's eyes. It was their sin and nobody else's.

When I got my speeding ticket that day, I was afraid that my dad wouldn't ever trust me again to drive his car, so I tried to pin the blame for my failure on everything else. I tried blaming the police officer for being too harsh and not letting me off with a warning. I tried to blame traffic which was holding me up and making me late. I even tried blaming my ticket on the bird that I ran over on my way to pick him up! Yes, I hit and killed a bird after leaving my house and attempted to shift the blame for my speeding that day to my frustration over the bird slaying. And I would have gone on and probably tried to blame the devil for giving me trouble or God for even allowing it! That is, except for the fact that my father stopped me and lovingly encouraged me to take responsibility.

God encouraged Adam and Eve to do the same. He took them to task for their sin and pinned them down. He did not do it in a harsh or vindictive way, but he did do it firmly. As any loving parent would do, God didn't let them get away with their excuses. He pressed in on them individually until they caved in and confessed. Both of them ultimately confessed their sin when they finally admitted that they ate the fruit.

God really does us a favor by telling us in advance that we are not going to get away with sin. The story of creation shows us that God knows our sins and will hold us accountable for them. That way we don't have to waste time running, hiding, or deflecting. Trying to blame others for our mistakes is not going to work. God is not going to fall for it. Blaming others or even our circumstances for our failures will not fix the problems we have created. The only thing we can do to remedy our mistakes is to stop shifting them and start owning them. Instead of passing the buck or pointing the finger, we must take responsibility for our mistakes and learn from them.

There is a story about Sir Arthur Conan Doyle, who once decided to play a practical joke on one of his friends. He decided to send him a telegram which read, "Flee at once. All is discovered!" With twenty-four hours of receiving the note, the friend disappeared and was never heard from again.[33] The question for all of us is, what would we do if we got a letter like that? Would we flee or face the music? The Bible tells us that if we do not try to hide or shift the blame to others but instead just admit and confess our sin, there is abundant forgiveness and cleansing for us. In 1 John 1:8–9 we read, "If we say we have no sin, we deceive ourselves, and the truth is not in us. If we confess [admit] our sins, he is faithful and just to forgive us our sins and to cleanse us from all unrighteousness."

DISCUSSION QUESTIONS

1. Why did Adam and his wife try to hide from God?

2. Why did God call to the man and not to the woman?

3. How should Adam have protected his wife?

4. How did Adam and his wife try to deflect responsibility?

5. What should we do about our sin rather than deflect it?

CHAPTER 9

GOD'S BLUEPRINT FOR OUR RECKONING

A man went out drinking one night with his buddies and got into a fight at a bar. Thankfully his wife was already asleep when he got home, so he slipped quietly into the bathroom to wash away the alcohol on his breath and bandage his bumps and bruises. He then carefully climbed into bed, thinking that he'd gotten away with it all. In the morning, he woke to find his wife standing over him looking stern and asking, "You went drinking and got into a fight last night, didn't you?"

"Of course not, honey," he said.

"Well, if you didn't, then who put all the Band-Aids on the bathroom mirror?"

The truth is that despite our sometimes pathetic and vain attempts to do so, we cannot and will not get away with our sin. The Bible tells us that nobody ever gets away with sin, not even Adam and Eve.

When I got my speeding ticket, I wasn't off the hook just because my dad forgave me. I still had to pay the fine and spend a Saturday in traffic school. Even though I wasn't shamed by my father for my mistake, he didn't try to shield me from the reality of the consequences for my actions. He explained to me that I would still need to pay the traffic fine out of my savings account and attend traffic school in order to avoid getting points on my license. Though it was disappointing to spend so much of my hard-earned allowance on a fine and waste a whole day in school, I knew that this judgment was fair and appropriate. I needed to appreciate that there are consequences for my bad choices, and it was better for me to learn that lesson then before life got more complicated and the consequences became more costly.

You might have made some mistakes. Maybe you've made a lot of mistakes. Those mistakes are often accompanied by consequences that are unavoidable. Though God forgives and loves us through our failures, he does not often prevent us from experiencing the cost of our failures. In fact, it is very unusual that God will intervene to stop the inevitable effects of our choices. Whatever sins you've committed, you should know that though there is forgiveness from God, there are still real and sometimes painful consequences that God will either allow or cause to occur in your life.

In the creation story we find out that God judges the sin of Satan, Adam, and Eve and actually curses them for their betrayal. Now, when we hear the word "curse," we probably think of witches and voodoo dolls, waving wands and casting spells in order to inflict unspeakable pain and suffering onto others. But that is not the biblical picture of curses. The Bible talks about blessings and curses not as magical incantations but as divine rewards and consequences that are justly doled out for certain kinds of behavior. Those who obey God and do his will are blessed with rewards and favor. Those who disobey God and betray him receive fair and appropriate penalties for their sins. Throughout the Old Testament, we see God deal with the people of Israel in this way, justly rewarding them when they follow his commands and disciplining them when they don't.

God has always dealt fairly with people and given them only what they rightfully deserve. One of the essential things about fair discipline is making sure the punishment actually fits the crime. In the case of the fall in the garden, God meted out judgment on the serpent, on Adam, and on Eve, but he did so in a balanced manner. He did not wipe them all off the face of the earth, though it would have been his prerogative to have done so. Instead of raining down fire from heaven on all three of his betrayers, he instead prescribed tailored consequences for each of them that matched their particular offense. In his pronouncements of judgment, we don't find any evidence of anger, spite, or resentment. Rather, we see that God is impartial, fair, and gentle in the way he handles and doles out verdicts.

This is significant because some people try to paint God as some sort of angry tyrant who smites anyone who threatens his rule or dares to disobey him. The caricature of God as a kind of moral monster has been popularized and promulgated in our culture, and many have used it as an excuse to jettison belief in God and reject matters of faith. Even though it is far from the truth, people continue to foster the false idea that God is somehow abusive and unfair in his judgment of the world. The truth is that God is nothing of the sort. What we see in the Scriptures is that God deals fairly and justly with people. He even dealt graciously with the serpent in the garden, even though it deserved no mercy. God does confront rebellion, and he does judge betrayal, but he always does it in the right way.

If you've carried around a caricature of God as an angry and punishing deity, then you've had the wrong idea. God isn't angry at you, and he doesn't want to punish you. He loves you, and he wants to forgive you. The God of creation is a merciful and gracious being who does everything in love. Even when he brings consequences to bear on our lives, he is always doing it with love. In fact, the Bible tells us that God *is* love. This means that everything he is and everything he does is defined and carried out in love. This even includes his judgment.

In the case of the serpent, God could have, and perhaps some say *should* have, totally destroyed it for its treachery. When it slithered into Adam and Eve's presence on that fateful day and taunted them with prideful deceit, it became responsible for the world's most famous crime. God had every reason to turn it into roadkill, but he held back. He had another plan for the creature, one that would take all of history to execute. It was a better and wiser way to deal with the snake, and it involved stripping the creature of its pride and ensuring its ultimate demise. When the serpent betrayed God, God cursed it with disgrace and with defeat.

Genesis 3:14 says, "The Lord God said to the serpent, 'Because you have done this, cursed are you above all livestock and above all beasts of the field; on your belly you shall go, and dust you shall eat all the days of your life.'" Because the serpent deceived the woman into sinning, God cursed the serpent with a twofold consequence. The first part of that consequence was humiliation. As a penalty for its part in the fall, God condemned the serpent to a place beneath all of the other creatures he had created. God consigned it to degradation on the earth. He said that the serpent would live under the feet of other creatures and be trampled upon for the rest of its existence.

Now, if you live in a place where there are snakes, you know how they slither along the ground and get run over by cars in the road and stepped on by hikers on trails. They do "eat the dust" of the ground because they live in the dirt. In fact, they usually live under it in burrows and holes. Snakes are ground-dwelling creatures, and that is the only way we have ever known them. But before the fall, we can presume they were different somehow. The Genesis account doesn't tell us what that difference was, so we are left to speculate. It may be that snakes were physically different before the fall and therefore were mobile in some other way, or it may simply be that they lived primarily in the trees and didn't move on the ground during that time. Whatever the case, something changed, and God forced the snake to live on the ground where it would be trampled by animals and eat dust for the rest of its existence.

The second part of the consequence for the serpent's sin was defeat. Not the kind of defeat that comes from losing a contest, but the kind that comes from entering into God's judgment. In Genesis 3:15 God said, "I will put enmity between you and the woman, and between your offspring and her offspring; he shall bruise your head, and you shall bruise his heel." We tend to think of bruises as a small bump or scrape on our skin, which is usually just a nuisance and minor inconvenience. So when we hear that God's judgment on the snake was a bruise, we might presume that God was letting the snake off lightly. But that is not the case. The idea of bruising the head of the serpent is a reference to God's holy judgment that would one day be doled out on the snake. What God is doing here is introducing the drama of the battle that would unfold between Christ and Satan in the future yet to come. This is the foreshadowing of how the Messiah would be "bruised" by Satan on the cross and how Satan would be "bruised" by Christ at the final judgment. The Scriptures are full of prophetic references, and many of them involve the coming of an anointed Messiah who would one day defeat evil and establish righteousness on earth. In other words, this Messiah (or "Christ" in Greek) would set right everything that went wrong in the garden. The story would come to a climactic conclusion with the ultimate judgment of evil and the devil who started it.

We read in Genesis 3:15 that God would put enmity between the "offspring" of the serpent and of the woman. Jesus would be the offspring of Adam and Eve, and Satan would be the offspring of the serpent, and both would be bruised. Satan would one day bruise Jesus at the cross, but Jesus would later bruise Satan at the final judgment. We know this because of what it says in Isaiah 53:5, where the prophet wrote, "He was wounded for our transgressions; he was *bruised* for our iniquities; upon him was the chastisement that brought us peace, and with his stripes we are healed." The bruise that Christ would suffer was only a bruise on the "heel" because he would rise from the dead after his crucifixion, but the bruise that Satan would suffer would be a bruise on the "head" because he would one day be totally defeated. In Romans 16:20 the apostle Paul writes, "The God of peace will soon crush Satan under your feet," which is a reference to this ultimate judgment upon the devil.

God first judged the serpent with disgrace and defeat, and then he turned his attention to Eve. God also judged the woman for her sin, and the curse he placed upon her was pain and envy. Again, it could have been a whole lot worse because she really did not deserve to live another day for her betrayal. And yet God was gracious with her and dealt fairly with her sinfulness.

The first part of the just consequence for her sin was increased pain in childbirth. From that point on, bearing children would become much more painful that it had been before. (I guess all the women in the world can send their thank-you notes to Eve for this lovely curse, because it is her fault.)

In Genesis 3:16 we read, "To the woman he said, 'I will surely multiply your pain in childbearing; in pain you shall bring forth children.'" But what does this mean? How exactly would the woman's pain increase in childbirth? It is interesting that the Hebrew word for "pain" is *etseb,* and it means "toil or labor." The verse literally says that because of her sin, God would increase the toil or labor of childbirth. It does not necessarily mean that her actual pain would increase but that the work or labor required would increase.

The second part of Eve's judgment was the curse of envy. Envy is jealousy or illegitimate desire. In Genesis 3:16 God says to her, "Your desire shall be for your husband, and he shall rule over you." The Hebrew word for "desire" is *teshukah,* and it means "craving or longing." Now, many misunderstand this and take it that the woman was being cursed with increased sexual desire. But that is not what it is saying. Sexual desire for one's spouse is *not* a curse. It is a blessing, and God is not talking about that here.

Instead, the word for "desire" in the Hebrew suggests something more like desire for domination or manipulation. The curse actually levied on the woman was that she would crave or long for control over her husband. We know this because of the way the same word is used in the very next chapter regarding the craving or longing of sin for us. Genesis 4:7 says, "If you do not do well, sin is crouching at the door. Its desire is for you, but you must rule over it." Therefore, the curse upon the woman is not increased sexual desire for her husband, but rather increased envy over his role as the leader of the family. As a result of the fall, she will want to buck the created order by trying to control and manipulate him.

This curse continues to haunt wives today, who sometimes struggle with wanting to unduly influence or even overpower their husbands. This is perhaps why the Bible speaks so much to the issue of biblical submission in marriage. There is a lot of emphasis in the Scriptures on charging women to submit to their husbands, and it makes sense that the reason for this is the curse of desire placed on women. God frequently reminds wives not to desire control over their husbands but rather to live gently and quietly with them. After all, in 1 Peter 3:4 it says to wives,

"Let your adorning be the hidden person of the heart with the imperishable beauty of a gentle and quiet spirit, which in God's sight is very precious."

So God first judged the serpent. Then he judged Eve. And finally, he judged Adam. God judged the man for his sin by cursing him with labor and with death. In Genesis 3:17 we read, "And to Adam he said, 'Because you have listened to the voice of your wife and have eaten of the tree of which I commanded you, "You shall not eat of it," cursed is the ground because of you; in pain you shall eat of it all the days of your life; thorns and thistles it shall bring forth for you; and you shall eat the plants of the field.'" Just as with Eve, the consequence for Adam is twofold. The first part of his curse is increased pain, but his pain would not be in childbearing but in working. Just as the woman's labor was increased and her toil lengthened, so was the man's. But his work would be the hard labor of toiling in the fields.

We read that as a result of the fall, the man will now have to "sweat" at his work. This seems funny in a way because it sounds as though the man never had to work hard enough to sweat before, but that is not really what is going on here. Sweating is not the point. I know people who sweat just sitting on the couch and others who don't sweat even in the gym. The real implication of this is that work that was once a blessing would now become a curse. In other words, the man would find that things he once found enjoyable would seem oppressive and exhausting. Yes, the work itself definitely increased, but the real "pain" was the lack of fulfillment and enjoyment that he would derive from it.

Men have the sense today that there's something right about work, but that something has gone wrong too. Work was designed to be a blessing, but it became a curse after the fall.

Men were created from the beginning to enjoy their work and to derive fulfillment from the things they do each day. But because of the consequence of sin, so many men now find themselves in jobs where they slave away and get little sense of the satisfaction they were made to enjoy. Before Adam sinned, work was a blessing for men, but after the fall it became toil. The emptiness that men feel in their work is there for a reason. It is a result of the curse of Adam that still lingers over them.

The other part of the curse for man was the ultimate disgrace, death. In Genesis 3:19 God said, "By the sweat of your face you shall eat bread, til you return to the ground, for out of it you were taken; for you are dust, and to dust you shall return." This is the ultimate consequence, because man was created to live and not to die. Most biblical scholars agree that God did not intend for people to die when he created them. He made them to live forever, but their sinfulness changed that plan. Because they ate of the forbidden fruit and now knew the difference between good and evil, they also became familiar with the consequences of evil. And the chief consequence for evil is death.

When Adam sinned, he brought death to himself, his family, and the entire human race. Because of his sin, death was introduced into a world where it should not have ever been. It spread in the world, and it spread quickly. The Scriptures tell us that Adam's death was also the death of all creation. Adam's sin resulted in a chain reaction of corruption and decay in everything God had created. Creation was reversing course, going backward toward chaos all over again. The consequence for Adam's sin brought the ultimate curse on all of creation because death spread through him to everyone and everything else. Romans 8:20–22 says, "For the creation was subjected to futility, not willingly, but because of him who subjected it, in hope that the creation itself will be set free from its bondage to decay and obtain the freedom of the glory of the children of God. For we know that the whole creation has been groaning together in the pains of childbirth until now."

The cost associated with Adam's sin was the curse of death, not just for him but for everyone else. If you have ever wondered why we even die in the first place, it's because of Adam's sin. Because he had a human nature, he was prone to make the wrong choices. He did. He sinned in his fallen nature, and because we have inherited his nature, we sin too. That means we die also. Sin leads to death. It's not only a consequence. It's an inevitable result of choosing to go our own way. When we think we know what's best for us, we often do our own thing and get ourselves into deep trouble. The Bible says that we are all like sheep who have gone astray, and lost sheep fall off cliffs and get eaten by wolves. They also get lost and starve to death.

Our sinfulness has created a death problem for all of us. Thankfully, though, God had a solution in the works even before Adam started to die. He had hatched a rescue plan for the world, and it involved a Rescuer. In the fifth chapter of Romans we see that Adam was a type of someone else who was to come. A type is a shadow or forerunner of another person. Paul tells us that this person was Jesus Christ. Where Adam failed, Jesus would prevail. He in his death on the cross would remedy the curse of death by dying for justification and life. In other words, Adam's sinfulness is what imperiled the world, but Jesus's righteousness is what redeemed it. In Romans 5:12, 18, it says, "Therefore just as sin came into the world through one man, and death spread through sin, and so death spread to all men because all sinned… Therefore, as one trespass led to condemnation for all men, so one act of righteousness leads to justification and life for all men."

Even though we see in the creation story that God has to

judge creation, we know from the gospel story that he really wants to save it. In other words, even though we deserve death, God prefers life. The truth is that God never wanted to judge anyone. God had to judge the serpent, the woman, and the man because he is just. God's justice required him to curse sin, but we also see that his love motivated him to overcome it. From the beginning, God wanted to have eternal and unbroken fellowship with us, so he was willing to put a plan into action in order to redeem and restore that fellowship. In John 3:16–17, Jesus said, "God so loved the world, that he gave his only Son, that whoever believes in him should not perish but have eternal life. For God did not send his Son into the world to condemn the world, but in order that the world might be saved through him."

DISCUSSION QUESTIONS

1. How is the gospel revealed in the curse upon the serpent?

2. How does desire become a curse for the woman?

3. How is the ground cursed because of the man's sin?

4. What kind of death is the consequence for his sin?

5. What did God do to reverse the curse of death?

CHAPTER 10

GOD'S BLUEPRINT FOR OUR REDEMPTION

The ancient philosopher Thomas Aquinas proposed that three things are necessary for the salvation of man: to know what he ought to believe; to know what he ought to desire; and to know what he ought to do.[34] Yes, salvation involves not just believing what is true but desiring it as well. But salvation ultimately is also about knowing what to do. The Bible tells us that there is something we have to do in order to get right with God. We can know God's truth, even desire it, but if we don't do something about it, then it is all really in vain. It is just information transfer that does not change anything. Belief must be validated by action. In other words, faith must be proven through something called repentance.

The Bible talks a lot about repentance. In the New Testament, the Greek word for repentance is *metanoia,* and it literally means to change one's mind—but it suggests not just a change of perspective but a change of direction. In other words, it means not just to think differently but to actually *go* in a new direction. In the case of fallen human beings, it is the choice to turn around and go back. But back to what? The answer is to go back to the Creator who made us. In the beginning, God made everything, and the capstone of his creation was human beings. Adam and Eve were the "very good" of creation. And God's greatest gift to humanity was freedom, the freedom to choose between serving

God and serving themselves. Initially, the man and woman served God, but once they were presented with the opportunity to choose otherwise, they did. They sinned when they exercised their freedom to disobey God and ended up not only desecrating the human race but also severing its union with God. What once was beautiful and peaceful was upended by ugly sin and moral anarchy.

Repentance is the personal choice to turn from sin and return to God. And that is what the man and woman did after they had betrayed God in the garden. The culmination of the creation story is not really the fall but the redemption of Adam and Eve. Though they sinned and were cursed for it, we see that they quickly recognized their mistakes and came back to God. Thankfully, they did not languish in their guilt or run away from their Creator. They could have fallen down and given up after failing so badly, but they didn't. They could have languished in despair or even run further away, but they made the right choice to turn back. In repenting, they accepted their consequences and moved on with life. Though they had to leave the garden and the world they had come to love, they did not give up on living.

We know this because of what we read immediately after they sinned and God judged them. It is critically important to note that the first thing Adam did after hearing his verdict was to name his wife, and the name he gave to her really says it all. It says in Genesis 3:20 that "The man called his wife's name Eve, because she was the mother of all living." That would be an odd way to respond to their failure if Adam had in fact given up after his sin. If their situation was so dire and they had no future, why would he have immediately named his wife "Mother of the Living"? Mother of the Dead might have been more fitting given their predicament. The fact that Adam chose a name about living has much so say about his response to their sins. It suggests that Adam had faith and that his faith had not been crushed by his failure. Whatever consequences he deserved, he was willing to accept. But that did not stop him from believing that God still had a plan for them and their descendants.

Indeed, God did still have a plan. So Adam named his wife Eve for the very reason that she would be the mother of all those who would live in the future. It is significant that Adam did not give his wife a generic description or leave her unnamed as "Woman." He could have done that. After all, Adam actually never gave himself a name. His "name" is Man, and that never changed. Biblical scholars believe that the naming of Eve is significant because it communicates that there was still hope for the human race. "Eve" in the Hebrew is *kavah,* and it means "life or living." Adam's choice of name for her does not just describe her role as childbearer but actually prescribes it, thus affirming her position at the top of the family tree of the human race. She would be the one through whom future children would be born and the earth would ultimately be filled. And the naming of his wife shows that Adam believed in God's promise. In his cursing of the serpent, God promised that one of her descendants would one day bruise it on the head, and Adam's response here shows that he believed this would come true. One day God would give them a descendant who would defeat Satan and make everything right. Adam's naming of Eve is important because it is essentially his act of repentance and profession of saving faith in God.

The evidence of Adam's repentance and profession is the sacrifice he offered. It says in Genesis 3:21 that "The Lord God made for Adam and for his wife garments of skins and clothed them." We read here that after Adam trusted God in faith, he substantiated his repentance with a sacrifice. The fact that God made them "garments of skins" shows that animals had to have died. Obviously, there were no fake furs back then, so those skins had to come from the hides of sacrificed animals. We can presume that Adam performed the first animal sacrifice in the Old Testament. Blood sacrifices are a prevalent theme throughout the Old Testament, and they were used to cover sins. What we understand is that these blood sacrifices, which usually involved bulls, lambs, or birds, were sufficient to temporarily cover sins but insufficient to actually cleanse them. In this sense, blood sacrifices were only provisional in nature until the final atoning sacrifice could be made.

We now know that the final sacrifice made to atone for sins was the death of Jesus Christ on the cross, which the Bible identifies as God's ultimate and final provision for the cleansing of all sins. We read in the book of Hebrews how this all happened. Hebrews 10:1–18 says, "For since the law has but a shadow of the good things to come instead of the true form of these realities, it can never, by the same sacrifices that are continually offered every year, make perfect those who draw near...For it is impossible for the blood of bulls and goats to take away sins... When Christ had offered for all time a single sacrifice for sins, he sat down at the right hand of God...For by a single offering he has perfected for all time those who are being sanctified... Where there is forgiveness of these, there is no longer any offering for sin." God's plan for redemption of sinners was to provide a system that would provisionally cover the sins of people for a time until a Savior would ultimately cleanse their sins through his sacrifice on the cross. This is God's rescue plan for sinners, and it is revealed in the third chapter of Genesis!

Many people think that the gospel message of forgiveness of sins is primarily a New Testament teaching. In other words, they have been led to believe that the gospel was introduced by

Jesus's disciples and was largely unknown before them. However, we see that God's salvation plan was actually unveiled in the very first book of the Bible, within the creation story itself. The entire sacrificial system that provides the framework for all the Hebrew Scriptures is entirely about the gospel. It was given to the world as the ultimate blueprint of God's plan for human beings, to lead them to the gospel truth about the Messiah and his atoning death on the cross. That means the gospel is the thread that ties the entire Bible together, and with it, all of human history!

Do you know what this means? It means that God himself always had a plan—a plan to redeem the world and to redeem you! This isn't just God's rescue plan for the world. It's God's rescue plan for *you!* The gospel is the reality that God has enabled our forgiveness by sending his Son Jesus to die on the cross in our place. If you and I repent of our sins by asking God to forgive us, he promises to save us. If you have been languishing in your sins and wondering what you can do about them, give them over to God and let him take them all away. God's plan for you has always been to redeem what has been lost and to restore what has been broken in your life.

God introduced his plan to Adam and Eve by enabling his forgiveness of them through instituting the first sacrifice. Notice that the purpose of that sacrifice was in order to "clothe them." This also is important, because it tells us a lot about God's providential care and concern for human beings. Whereas they had previously only had loincloths for covering, God now made tunics for them to wear. These tunics likely reached all the way down to their knees or ankles, providing cover over their entire bodies. The reason for this modest attire was to provide cover for their shame. In other words, God did something for Adam and Eve that they could not do for themselves. They were unable to do anything to cover their own guilt, but God in his loving care and concern did it for them. The beauty of this is that God does the same for us. We are also unable to do anything about our own guilt and shame for our sin, but God in his love has provided the means to cover it for us.

And yet, despite God's kind provision and Adam and Eve's humble repentance, there is still the reality that there are lingering consequences for their sins. It is so interesting to see that within the creation story, the people repent and God forgives them, but God does not intervene to stop the inevitable consequences that follow their failures. In other words, though God forgave them by providing the means to cover and ultimately cleanse their sins, he did not stop the decay and inevitable death that came as a result of their sins. In Genesis 3:22–23 we read, "Then the Lord God said, 'Behold, the man has become like one of us in knowing good and evil. Now, lest he reach out his hand and take also of the tree of life and eat and live forever'—therefore, the LORD God sent him out from the garden of Eden to work the ground from which he was taken." There were still unavoidable physical consequences that would come. And one of those inevitable consequences was mortality.

The curse of mortality shows us that there is a price to be paid for the loss of innocence. Even though Adam and Eve were forgiven, they not only lost their innocence but their lives. We read that God said, "Behold, the man has become like one of us," which means that Adam and Eve had tried to secure something that did not belong to them. Though they were human beings, they had tried to become something more. God could not allow that to happen. When Adam and Eve ate the fruit from the tree of knowledge of good and evil, they were warned they would die because they could not be like God. As created beings, they were intrinsically different from God by design, and it had to stay that way.

The inevitable consequence of sin was mortality, and mortality also meant exile. Exile, according to the dictionary, is the banishment or expulsion of someone from their home by authoritative decree. God exiled Adam and Eve from the garden of Eden because of their sin. They could not stay in paradise anymore because they had violated the conditions for living in the garden. Genesis 3:23–24 tells us that, "Therefore the Lord God sent him out from the garden of Eden to work the ground from which he was taken. He drove out the man, and at the east of the garden of Eden he placed the cherubim and a flaming sword that turned every way to guard the way to the tree of life." We read that God "sent" and "drove" them out of paradise, which was the painful result of the reality they now lived in. Rather than enjoying the peace of rest in the garden, they now had to go "work the ground" in the dry and dangerous lands outside of the sanctuary. This kind of life was going to be much harder and more unpleasant, and it would serve as a daily reminder of what they had given up. In order to keep them out of the garden, God stationed angels as guards and a flaming sword that would stop them if they ever tried to return. Their exile was irreversible. They could never return, and they could never come home. Their exile was a one-way ticket out of paradise into the real world, a world that was full of danger, difficulty, and deception. The world outside of that garden was the sad reality of life outside the blessing of God. Everything there was corrupted and displaced by sin, and life in that world would be far from God.

Many of us know all too well what life is like in the real world. We know the pain, the misery, and the hopelessness of living in a broken and fallen world. Ever since the garden, we have been wandering outside of God's perfect paradise. We have been stumbling and fumbling our way through life separated from the God who created and loves us. If God feels distant to you, it is because you've been going it alone in this world, trying to do it all yourself. But the reality is that we can't make it on our own. We need God. We need his presence. We need his love.

Adam and Eve's consequence for their sinfulness was to leave the presence of God in the garden and go it alone in the world outside. In the safety of the garden they had shared complete intimacy with God and enjoyed his presence every day, but that would now change. Because of their sin, they would have to leave the comfort of God's presence and live at a distance from him. The reality is that God could not fellowship with sinners and had to send them away. It's not that God abandoned them. It's that God had to distance himself from sinful beings. The reason for Adam and Eve's separation is still the reason for ours today.

The Bible says that sin is what separates us from God and keeps us from experiencing his presence today. The reason that God feels so far away is that our sin requires it. He has to stay away from us until we do something about our sin. So then, what can we do? The Scriptures tell us that in order to get close to God, we have to repent. What does repentance look like? James gives us a pretty clear description of it in James 4:7–10, where he says, "Submit yourselves therefore to God. Resist the devil, and he will flee from you. Draw near to God, and he will draw near to you. Cleanse your hands, you sinners, and purify your hearts, you double-minded. Be wretched and mourn and weep. Let your laughter be turned to mourning and your joy to gloom. Humble yourselves before the Lord, and he will exalt you." Repentance is turning your back on sin and selfishness and returning to God in humility and brokenness. James says that if we go back to God in this way, then he will come and meet us.

The Bible calls Jesus Christ the mediator between God and mankind, so meeting God in the middle means going through Jesus. In the Gospels Jesus calls himself the door, the gate, and the way to eternal life, and he is clear that there is no other way. Because Jesus is the Christ that the Father sent into the world in order to provide forgiveness of sins, he is the One we must go to and go through in order to have a restored relationship with our Creator. It is as Jesus said in John 14:6: "I am the way, the truth, and the life. No one comes to the Father except through me." Acts 4:12 says, "There is salvation in no one else, for there is no other name under heaven given among men by which we must be saved." Jesus is God's answer to the problem of sin. He is the Rescuer the Father sent into the world to right what went wrong in the garden and to mend the broken relationship between God and humanity.

I grew up in a Christian home, but I didn't truly grasp the meaning of what God did for me until I was a young adult. I will never forget hearing a pastor describe the anguish Jesus endured on the cross. He explained in excruciating detail how Jesus was beaten beyond recognition, pierced through with nails, and suffocated to death on that tree. He did all this while bearing the burden of everyone's sins, including mine and yours. Can you imagine how it must have felt to bear the weight and pain of every sin ever committed at once? I feel bad when I feel convicted about a single sin, let alone feeling every sin I've ever committed at the same time! And yet, Jesus did this. He suffered for us. He gave his life so we could have ours.

The good news of the gospel is that even though we are separated from God, we can be reconciled to him through Jesus

Christ. Paul tells us in Colossians 1:19–21, "In Christ all the fullness of God was pleased to dwell, and through him to reconcile to himself all things, whether on earth or in heaven, making peace by the blood of his cross. And you, who once were alienated and hostile in mind, doing evil deeds, he has now reconciled in his body of flesh by his death in order to present you holy and blameless and above reproach before him." According to this, we can close the gap between us and God by being reconciled with God through Jesus. By accepting and trusting in Christ as God's Son, we are choosing to reconcile with the Creator who made and loves us. This restoration of relationship is God's redemption plan for you and me.

The pastor and author A.B. Simpson once summed up God's great rescue plan for the whole world, writing, "The gospel tells rebellious men that God is reconciled, that justice is satisfied, that sin has been atoned for, that the judgment of the guilty may be revoked, the condemnation of the sinner cancelled, the curse of the Law blotted out, the gates of hell closed, the portals of heaven opened wide, the power of sin subdued, the guilty conscience healed, the broken heart comforted, the sorry and misery of the Fall undone!"[35]

DISCUSSION QUESTIONS

1. How did Adam and Eve respond to their sin?

2. How did God show forgiveness toward them?

3. Why are there still consequences for their sin?

4. What does God do to provide for their redemption?

5. How can we be reconciled with God?

CONCLUSION

N ow that you have seen God's blueprint, what will you do with it? Will you put this book on the shelf and just go back to the way things were, or will you put it to good use and make positive changes in your life? A blueprint, after all, is not helpful unless it is actually followed. It's important that you not only understand but also appreciate God's blueprint for your life. God has a master plan for you, for your family, your marriage, your job, your enjoyment, and your future, but you have to follow it if you want to experience all God has intended for you.

Don't ignore God's blueprint. Following it is essential for finding real satisfaction in this life. As we have seen, not following God's plan only leads to inevitable frustration, heartache, and loss. You will always feel like something is wrong in your life, like something is missing or out of place, if you avoid it or don't stick to it. Perhaps you've already found this to be true. Maybe you've been trying to do things your own way and have been running into walls and falling off cliffs at every turn. This world has a way of always letting us down because it offers us nothing in terms of value, meaning, and purpose.

The truth is that the world doesn't have a blueprint. Our culture tells us that there is no overarching storyline for the world, that there is no Creator who made us, and that there is nothing especially unique about human beings. As Peter Kreeft wrote in his book *Back to Virtue,* "There is a deep spiritual sorrow at the heart of modern civilization because it is the first civilization in all of history that does not know who it is or why it is, that cannot answer the three great questions: Where did I come from? Why am I here? And Where am I going? This is the most terrifying thing of all to us, because our primary need is denied, our need for meaning."[36]

In a world devoid of God, there is no meaning. There is no intrinsic purpose in anything or inherent value for any of us. Rather, we are taught by our culture that the only meaning to be found in this life is through making something of ourselves. "Be somebody," we are told. We hear that becoming somebody is achieved through personal success, wide notoriety, and accumulation of wealth. The truth is that this kind of blueprint is no blueprint at all because it doesn't work. It doesn't answer our questions, and it doesn't satisfy.

God does have a blueprint for us, and it tells us that our value, our identity, and our purpose has nothing to do with the things we achieve, with how attractive we are, or with how much stuff we have. It is not based upon our appearance or our performance. It is rooted in the simple fact that we bear God's image. As God's image bearers, we not only have immeasurable value; we also have undeniable purpose. God's blueprint for you and me is a plan for our fulfillment in this life, and all we have to do is follow it. In other words, our flourishing as human beings has everything to do with simply sticking to God's plan.

After reading this book, you may realize that you need to make some critical changes in your life in order to align with God's plan. Perhaps you need to take more leadership in your family or make a change at your job. Maybe you need to establish better boundaries in your life or accept responsibility for a mistake. It may be that you need to stop listening to the voice of low self-esteem and start claiming your image in God. Whatever the changes might be, I challenge you to have the courage to make them, even if they are hard. If you believe that God's way is best and that it brings the most blessing, then choose his plan and stick to it. Take this blueprint. Use it. Follow God's design, and experience the kind of life you were created to live.

ENDNOTES

Introduction

1. George Gaylord Simpson, *The Meaning of Evolution* (New Haven, CT: Yale University Press, 1967), 345.
2. Francis Schaeffer, *Death in the City* (Downers Grove, IL: InterVarsity Press, 1972), 18.

Chapter One

3. G.K. Chesterton, *St. Thomas Aquinas: The Dumb Ox* (Garden City, NY: Doubleday Image, 1974), 145.
4. Michael Gerson, "On Crying at the Movies," *Washington Post*, January 9, 2013.
5. Stephen Hawking and Leonard Mlodinow, *The Grand Design* (New York: Bantam Press, 2010), 180.
6. Matt Crenson, "'Smoking Gun' Suggests Instantaneous Expansion of Universe," *The Arizona Republic*, March 17, 2006.
7. Elizabeth Barrett Browning, "Aurora Leigh," *The Oxford Book of English Mystical Verse* (Nicholson & Lee, Eds., 1917), Book 7.
8. Quoted by Robert Johnston, *Reel Spirituality* (Grand Rapids, MI: Baker, 2000), 151.
9. John Mark Reynolds, "Beauty" (Lecture, Torrey Honors Institute at Biola University, La Mirada, CA, October 9, 2006).
10. Malcolm Muggeridge, *Christ and the Media* (London: Hodder & Stoughton, 1977), 25.

CHAPTER TWO

11. Thomas Molnar, "Jean-Paul Sartre, RIP: A Late Return," *National Review*, 34, no. 11 (June 11, 1982), 677.

12. Nevada Barr, *Seeking Enlightenment Hat by Hat: A Skeptic's Path to Religion* (New York: Berkeley Books, 2003), 17.

13. Chris Williams has a PhD in biochemistry and is developing a website at www.complexityoflife.com.

14. Steve Jones, *The Language of Genes* (New York: Anchor Books, 1993), 15.

15. C.S. Lewis, *The Weight of Glory and Other Addresses* (New York: HarperOne, 2001), 46.

16. J.I. Packer, *Your Father Loves You: Daily Insights for Knowing God* (Chicago: Harold Shaw Publishers, 1986) Feb. 23.

17. Thornton Wilder, *Our Town* (New York: HarperCollins, 2003), Act III, 87.

CHAPTER THREE

18. J.R.R. Tolkien, *Tree & Leaf: Mythopoeia* (San Francisco: HarperCollins, 2001), 87.

19. Madeleine L'Engle, *Walking on Water: Reflections on Faith and Art* (Wheaton, IL: Harold Shaw Publishers, 1980), 134.

20. Dorothy Sayers, *Mind of the Maker* (New York: Bloomsbury Publishing, 2005), 17.

21. Charles Dickens, *Sketches by Boz* (London: Penguin Classics, 1996), 238.

CHAPTER FOUR

22. Leonardo da Vinci, Irma Richter, Thereza Wells, and Martin Kemp, *Leonardo da Vinci: Notebooks* (Oxford: Oxford University Press, 2008), 209.

23. Blaise Pascal, *Pensees* (Whitefish, MT: Kessinger Publishing, 2004), 34.

24. Gordon McDonald, *Ordering Your Private World* (Nashville, TN: Thomas Nelson, 2007), 193.

Chapter Five

25. Jim Collins, *Good to Great* (New York, NY: HarperCollins, 2001), 210.

26. Marcus Wohlsen, "Facebook Billionaire Shuns Luxury for Startup Life," *Yahoo News*, April 29, 2012.

27. Christianity Today, "More Oxygen to the Flame: A conversation with Zig Ziglar and Ben Patterson," *Christianity today.com*, October 1, 1998, http://www.christianity today.com/le/1998/ fall/8l4020.html?start=2 (accessed January 20, 2013).

Chapter Six

28. Matthew Henry, *Matthew Henry's Commentary on the Whole Bible: Completed and Unabridged* (Peabody, MA: Hendrickson Publishers, 2008), 7.

29. Walter Wangerin, Jr., *As For Me and My House: Crafting Your Marriage to Last* (Nashville, TN: Thomas Nelson Publishers, 2001), 59.

Chapter Seven

30. John Milton, *Paradise Lost*, 12.84.

Chapter Eight

31. Inside Hoops, "Greatest NBA Quotes," http://www.inside-

hoops.com/forum/showthread.php?t=200746 (accessed January 25, 2013).

32. Philo of Alexandria, *The Contemplative Life, Giants and Selections* (Mahwah, NJ: Paulist Press, 1980), 181.

33. Editorial, "Men Met in the Hotel Lobbies," *The Washington Post*, June 16, 1901, 18.

CHAPTER TEN

34. Thomas Aquinas, *The Commandments of God: Conferences on the Two Precepts of Charity and the Ten Commandments* (London: Burns, Oates & Washbourne, 1937).

35. G. Michael Cocoris, *Evangelism: A Biblical Approach* (Chicago: Moody Press, 1984), 29.

CONCLUSION

36. Peter Kreeft, *Back to Virtue: Traditional Moral Wisdom for Modern Moral Confusion* (San Francisco: Ignatius Press, 1992), 156.

BIBLIOGRAPHY

Aquinas, Thomas. *The Commandments of God: Conferences on the Two Precepts of Charity and the Ten Commandments*. London: Burns, Oates & Washbourne, 1937.

Barr, Nevada. *Seeking Enlightenment Hat by Hat: A Skeptic's Path to Religion*. New York: Berkeley Books, 2003.

Browning, Elizabeth Barrett. "Aurora Leigh" *The Oxford Book of English Mystical Verse,* Book 7. Nicholson & Lee, Eds., 1917.

Chesterton, G.K. *St. Thomas Aquinas: The Dumb Ox.* Garden City, NY: Doubleday Image, 1974.

Cocoris, G. Michael. *Evangelism: A Biblical Approach.* Chicago: Moody Press, 1984.

Collins, Jim. *Good to Great.* New York, NY: HarperCollins, 2001.

Da Vinci, Leonardo, Irma Richter, Thereza Wells & Martin Kemp. *Leonardo da Vinci: Notebooks.* Oxford: Oxford University Press, 2008.

Dickens, Charles. *Sketches by Boz.* London: Penguin Classics, 1996.

Hawking, Stephen & Leonard Mlodinow. *The Grand Design.* New York: Bantam Press, 2010.

Henry, Matthew. *Matthew Henry's Commentary on the Whole Bible: Completed and Unabridged.* Peabody, MA: Hendrickson Publishers, 2008.

Johnston, Robert. *Reel Spirituality.* Grand Rapids, MI: Baker Publishing, 2000.

Jones, Steve. *The Language of Genes.* New York: Anchor Books, 1993.

Kreeft, Peter. *Back to Virtue: Traditional Moral Wisdom for Modern Moral Confusion.* San Francisco: Ignatius Press, 1992.

L'Engle, Madeleine. *Walking on Water: Reflections on Faith and Art.* Wheaton, IL: Harold Shaw Publishers, 1980.

Lewis, C.S. *The Weight of Glory and Other Addresses.* New York: HarperOne, 2001.

McDonald, Gordon. *Ordering Your Private World.* Nashville, TN: Thomas Nelson, 2007.

Milton, John. *Paradise Lost.* London: Penguin Classics, 2003.

Muggeridge, Malcolm. *Christ and the Media.* London: Hodder & Stoughton, 1977.

Packer, J.I. *Your Father Loves You: Daily Insights for Knowing God.* Chicago: Harold Shaw Publishers, 1986.

Pascal, Blaise. *Pensees.* Whitefish, MT: Kessinger Publishing, 2004.

Philo of Alexandria. *The Contemplative Life, Giants and Selections.* Mahwah, NJ: Paulist Press, 1980.

Reynolds, John Mark. "Beauty," Lecture, Torrey Honors Institute at Biola University, La Mirada, CA, October 9, 2006.

Sayers, Dorothy. *Mind of the Maker.* New York: Bloomsbury Publishing, 2005.

Schaeffer, Francis. *Death in the City.* Downers Grove, IL: InterVarsity Press, 1972.

Simpson, George Gaylord. *The Meaning of Evolution.* New Haven, CT: Yale University Press, 1967.

Tolkien, J.R.R. *Tree & Leaf: Mythopoeia.* San Francisco: HarperCollins, 2001.

Wangerin, Walter Jr. *As For Me and My House: Crafting Your Marriage to Last.* Nashville, TN: Thomas Nelson, 2001.

Wilder, Thornton. *Our Town.* New York: HarperCollins, 2003.

CONNECT WITH THE AUTHOR

www.kentdelhousaye.com
Email: kent@kentdelhousaye.com
Facebook: facebook.com/kdelhousaye
Twitter: twitter.com/kentdelhousaye